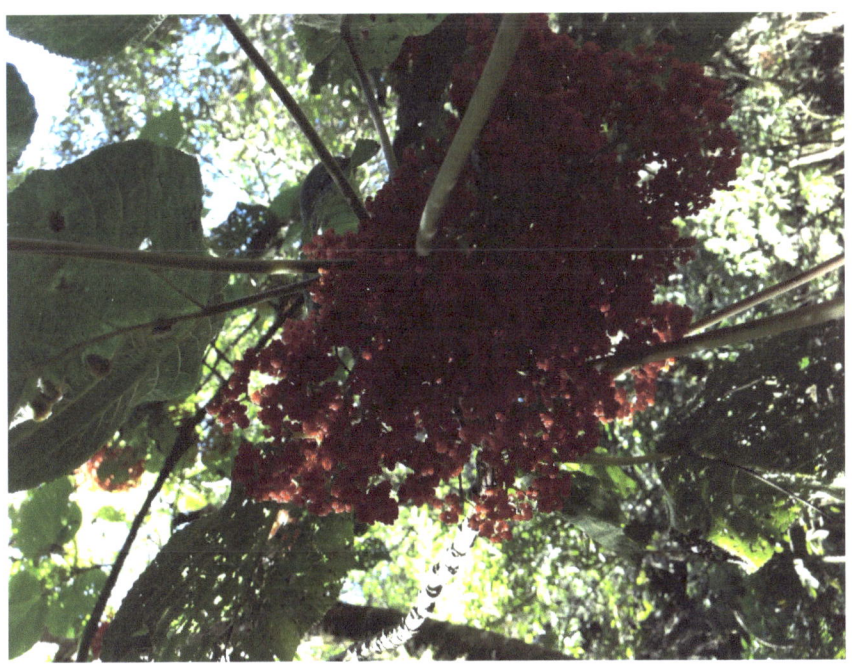

Nature Energy Vibes

Nature in a Different point of View

Tony Meyer DD

ISBN: 1500255238
ISBN-13: 978-1500255237

DEDICATION

I dedicate this book to planet Earth. We are all part of this amazing planet, home to everyone. No matter what country you live in, what country you love, or what country you were born in, they are all one, they are all planet Earth. We are all one, sharing the same roots and exchanging, constantly, energy between us and all our surroundings. So let this book be a reminder of who we are and how we got to be who we are and where we are. Let appreciate what is really important in life and forget what we don't really need, but want; all of this things which only break us and destroy us starting from the outside progressively moving to our inside.

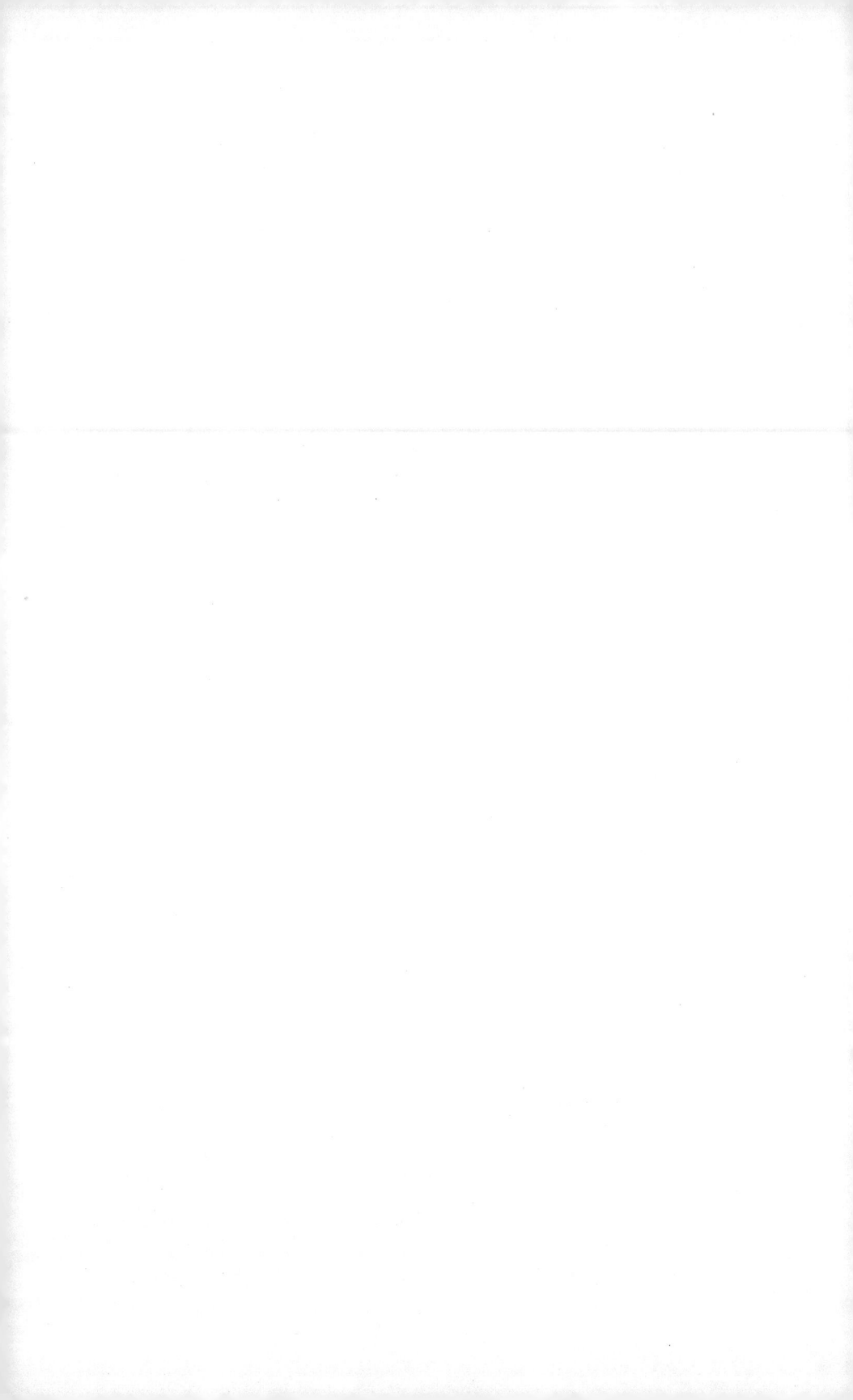

ACKNOWLEDGMENTS

I want to thank my family for supporting me throughout my whole life and my friends (I consider them as my brothers), for being with me in the journey of making this pictures, and sharing the message and the vibes of this pictures in many different ways.

Begin

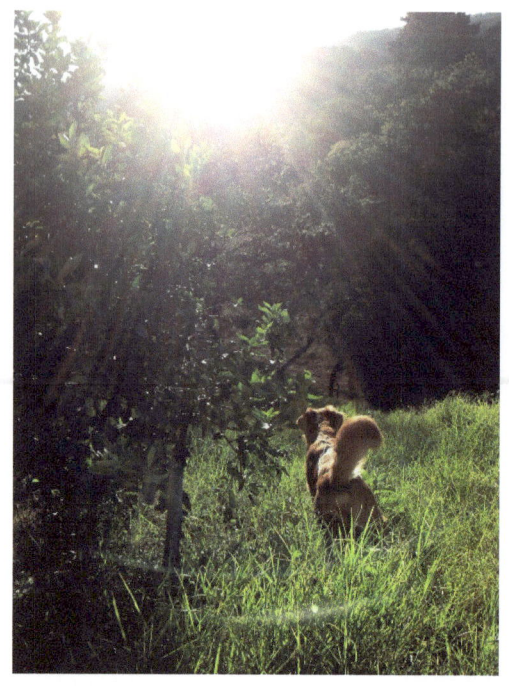

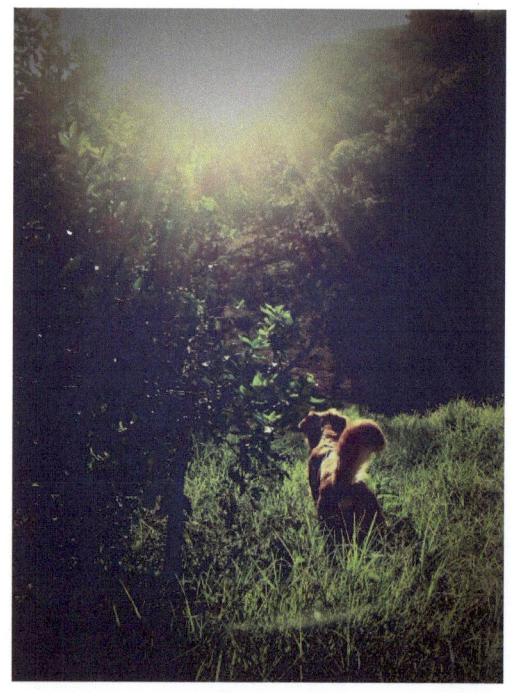

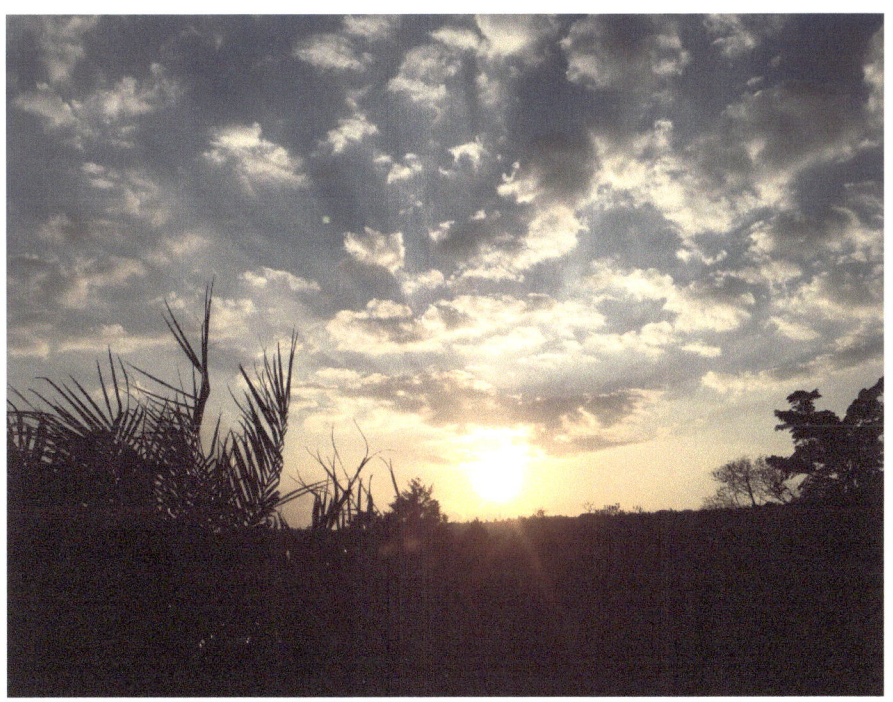

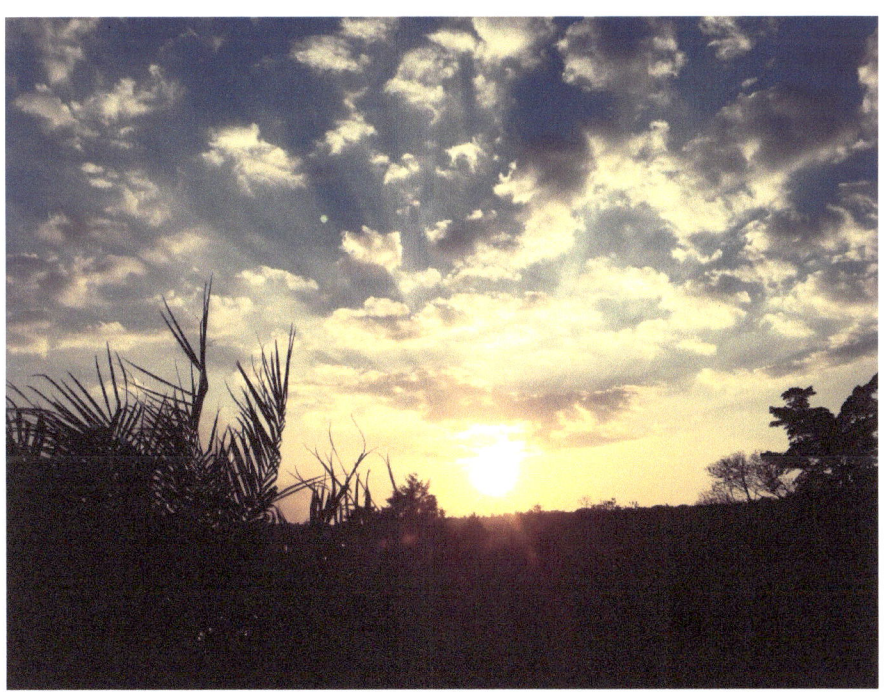

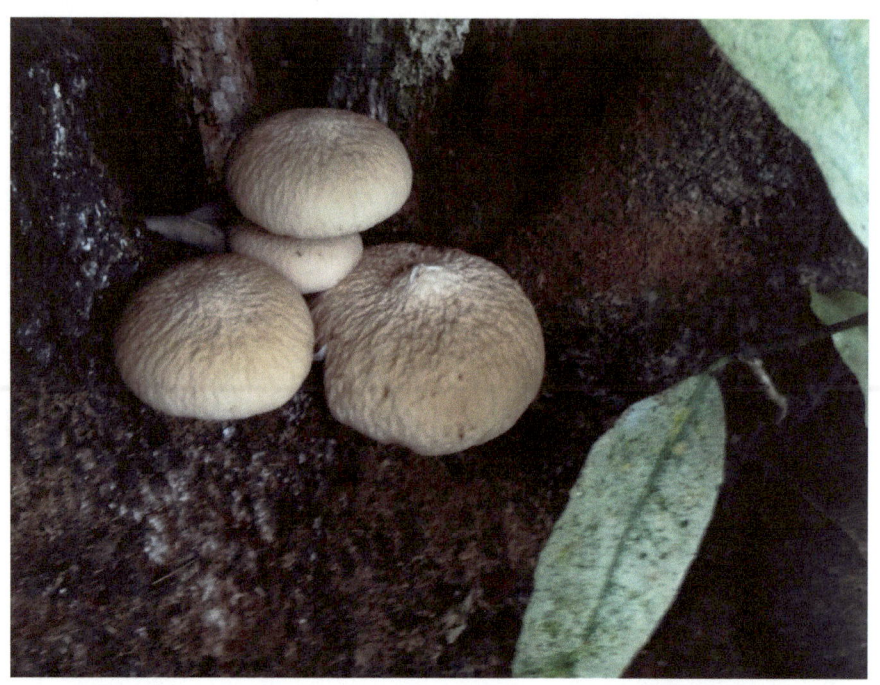

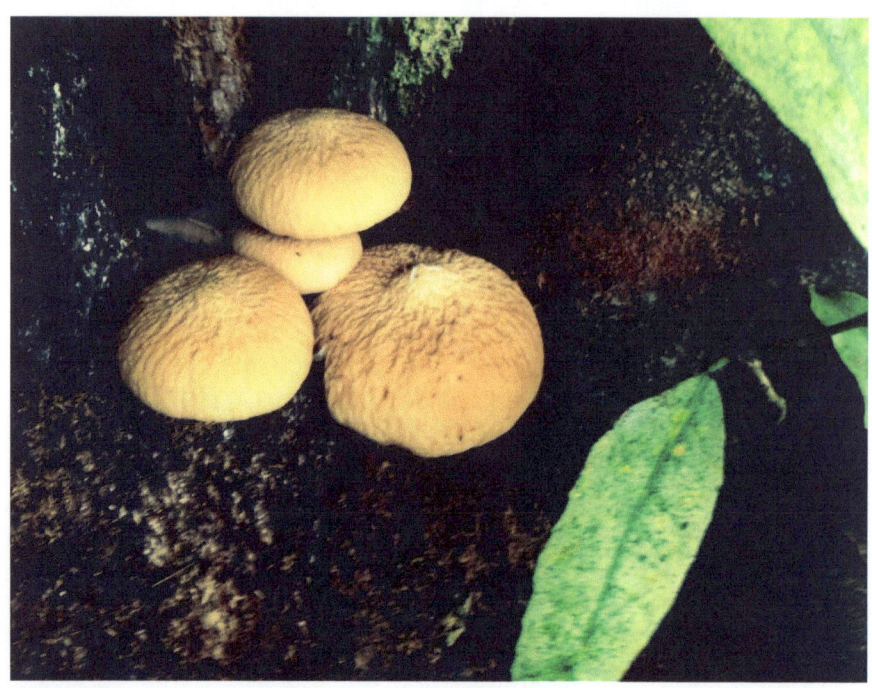

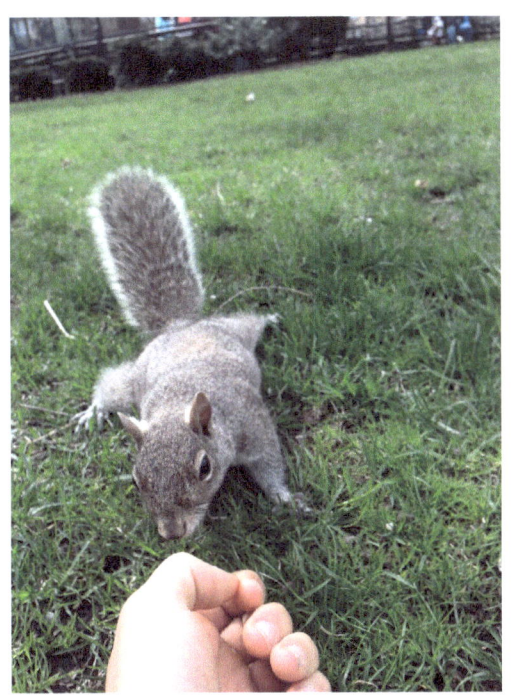

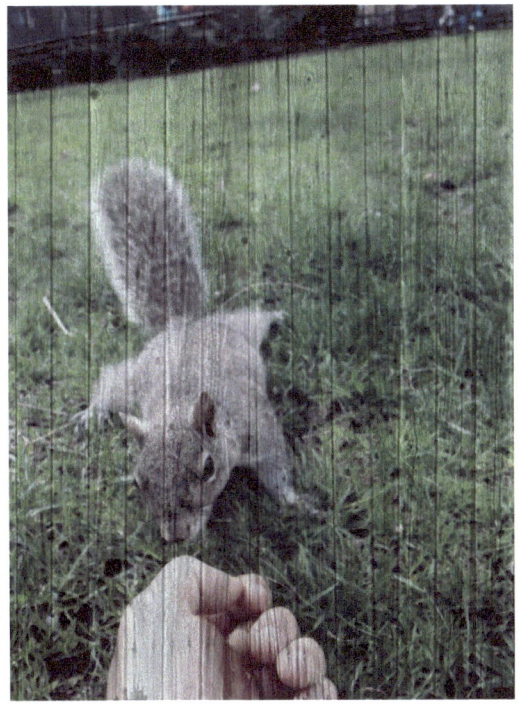

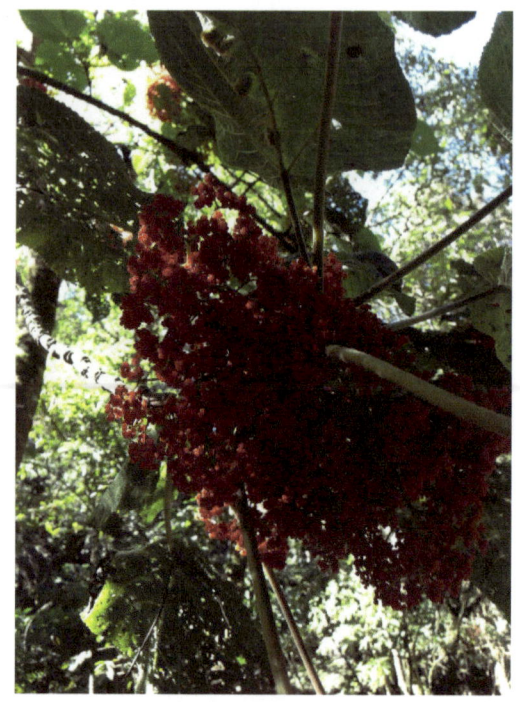

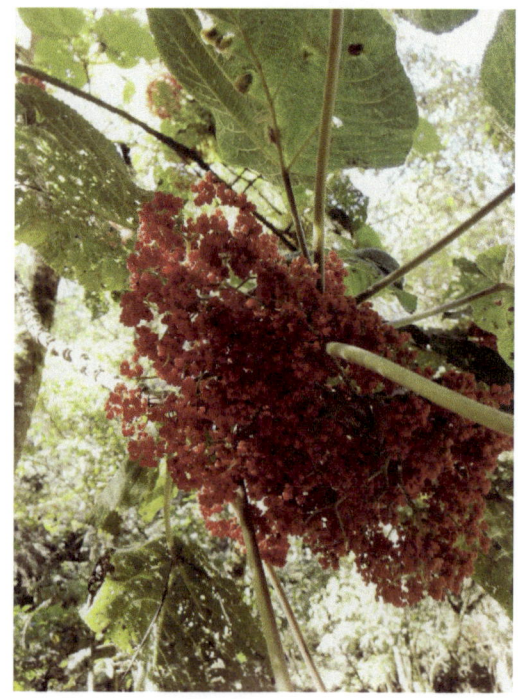

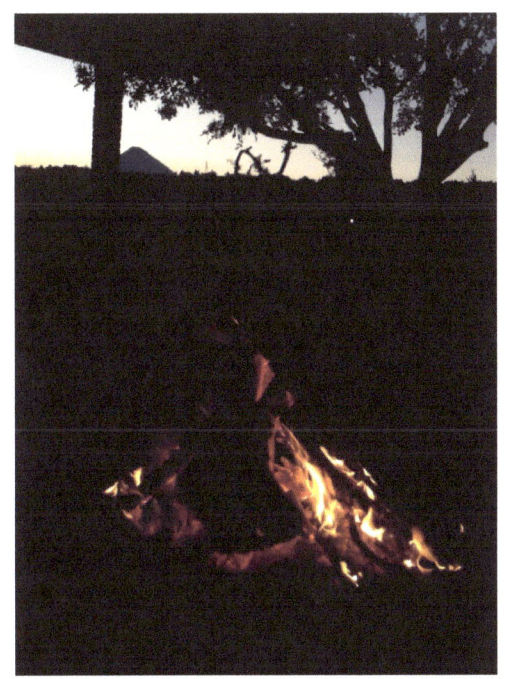

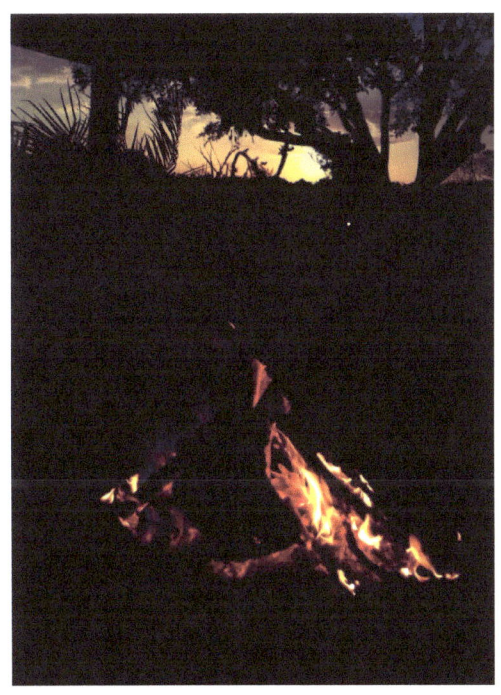

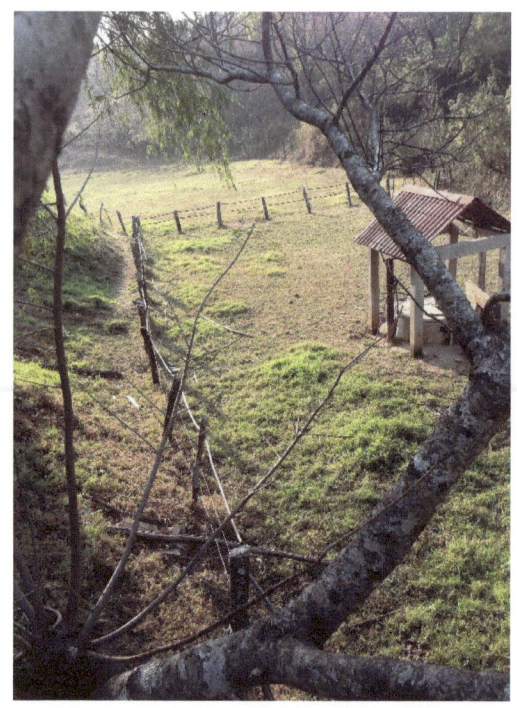

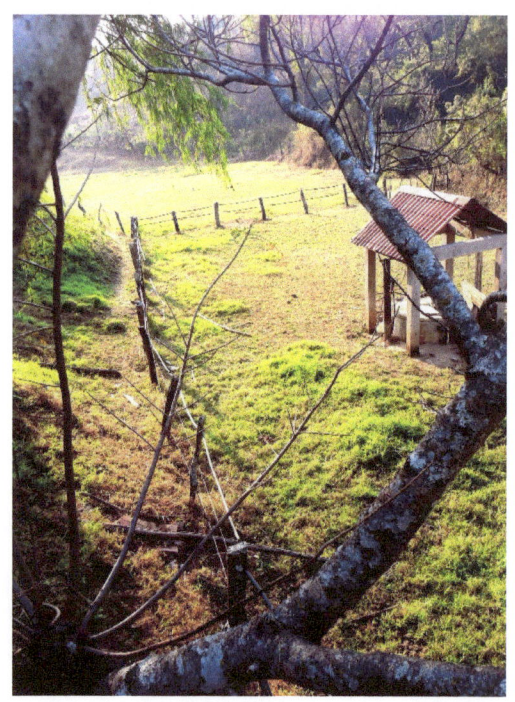

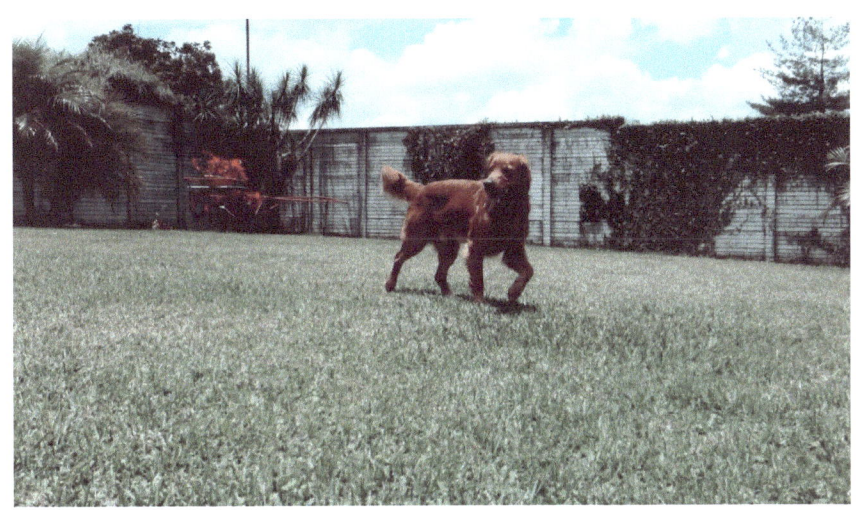

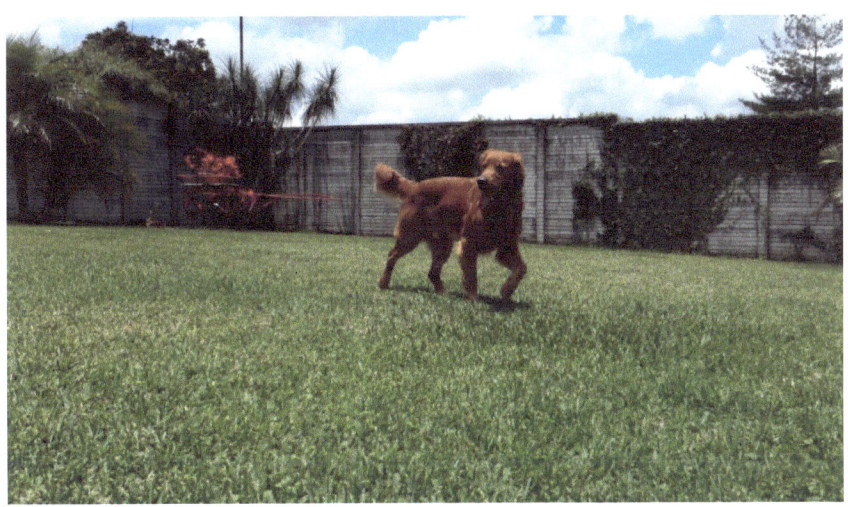

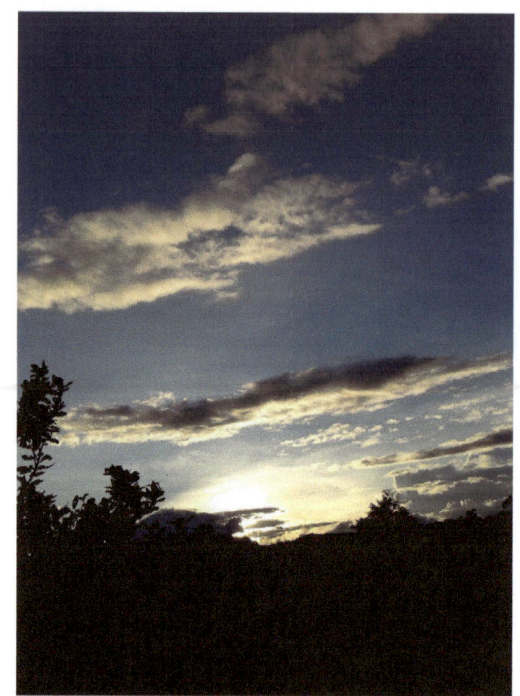

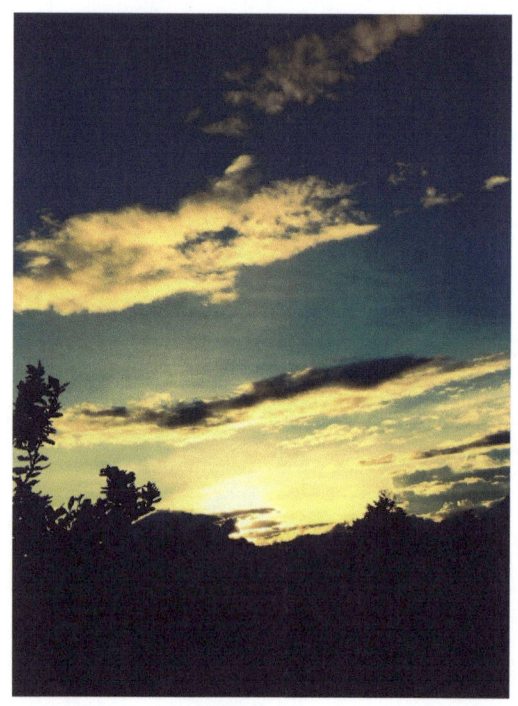

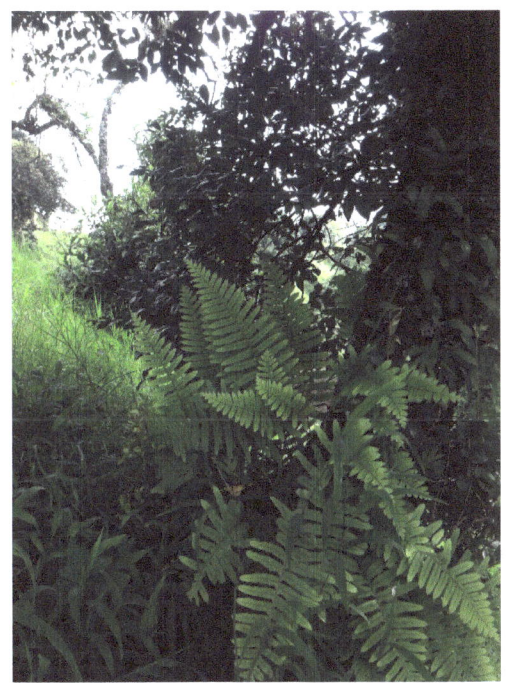

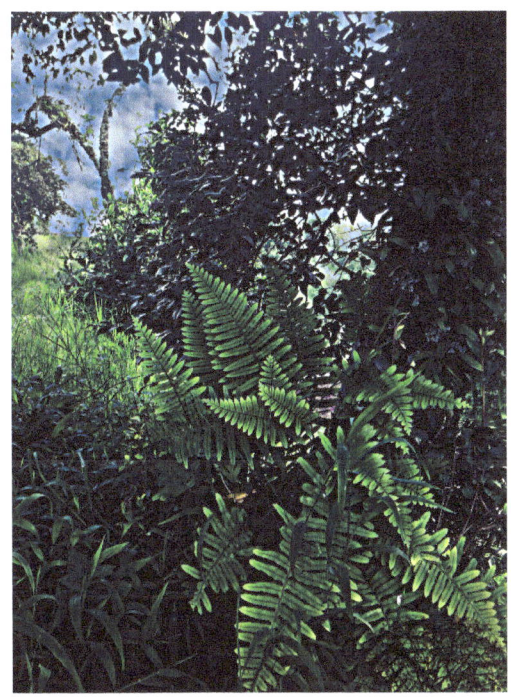

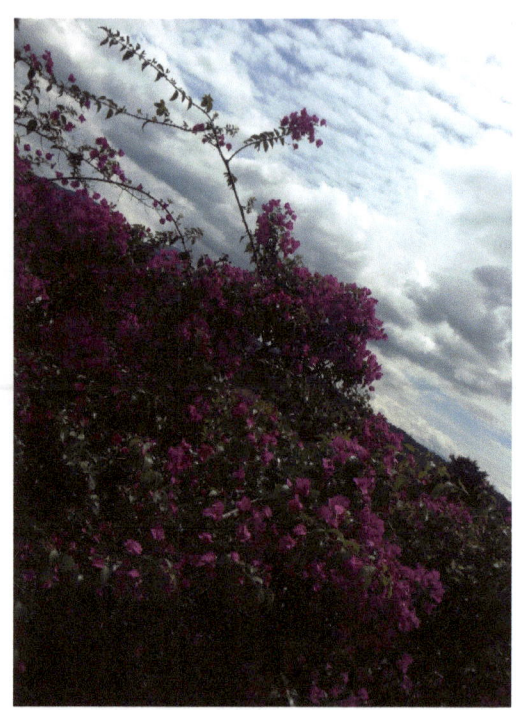

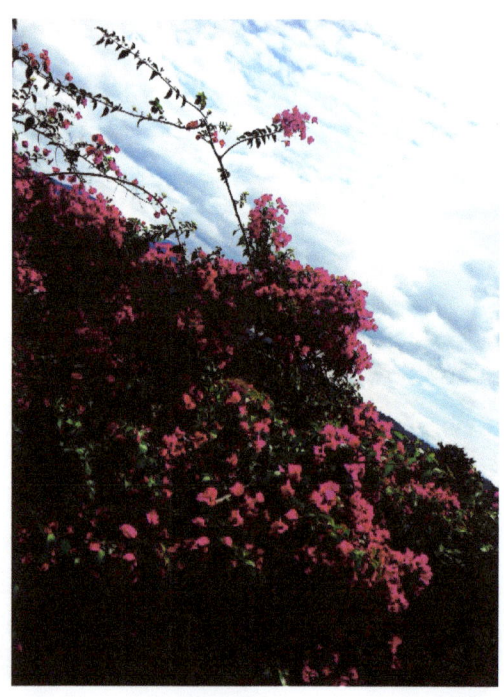

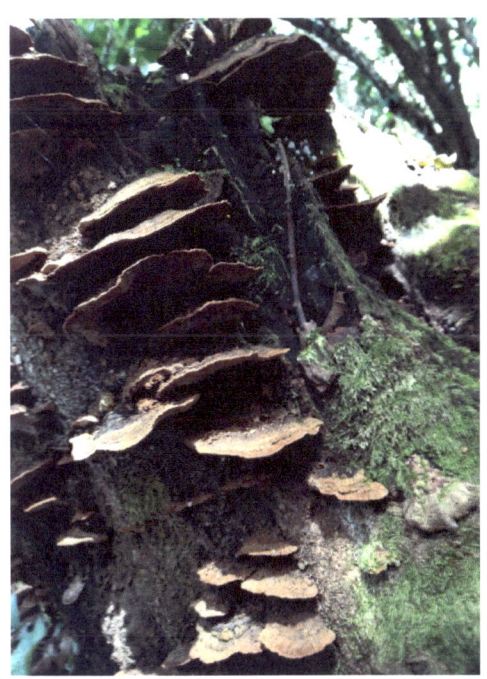

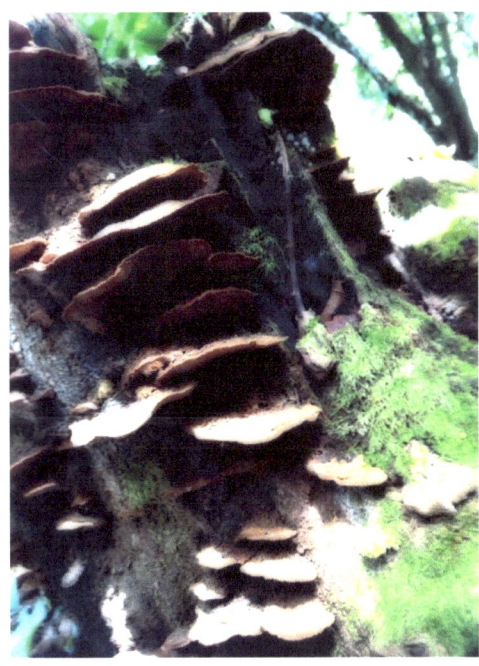

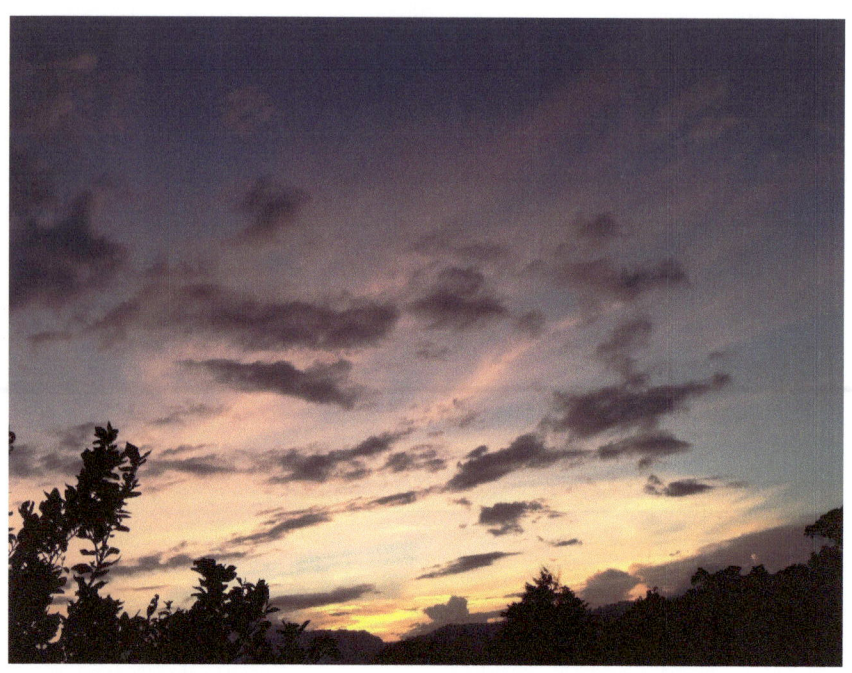

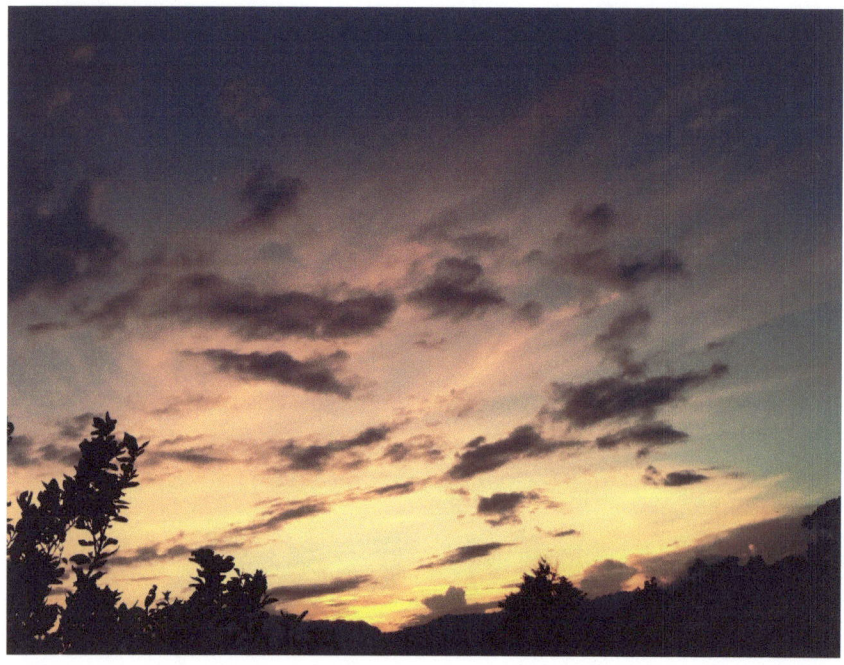

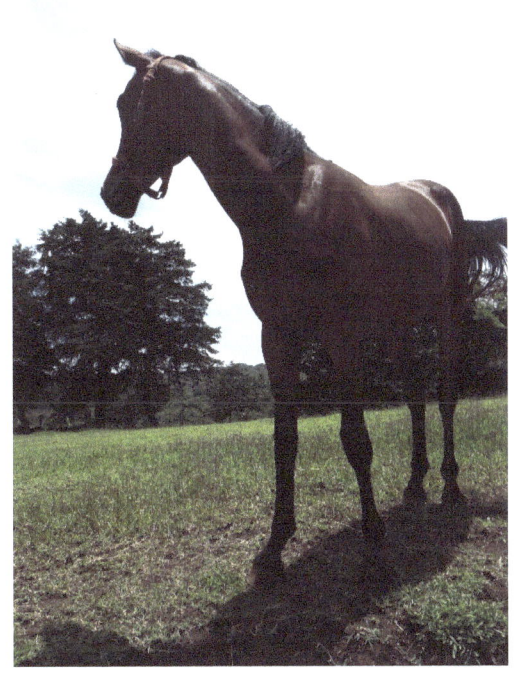

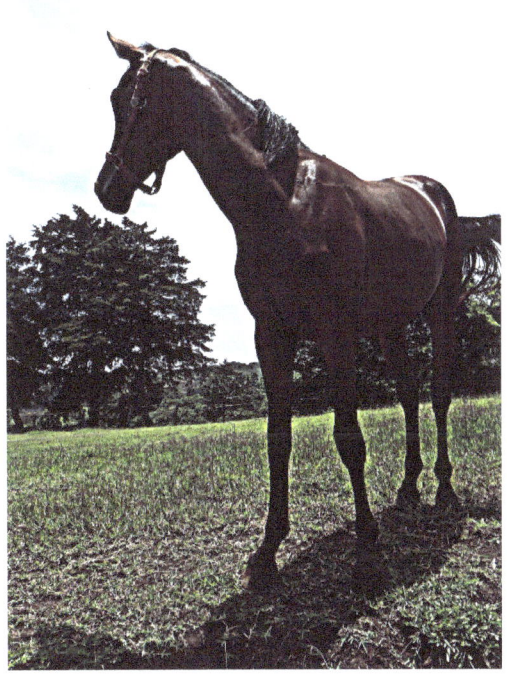

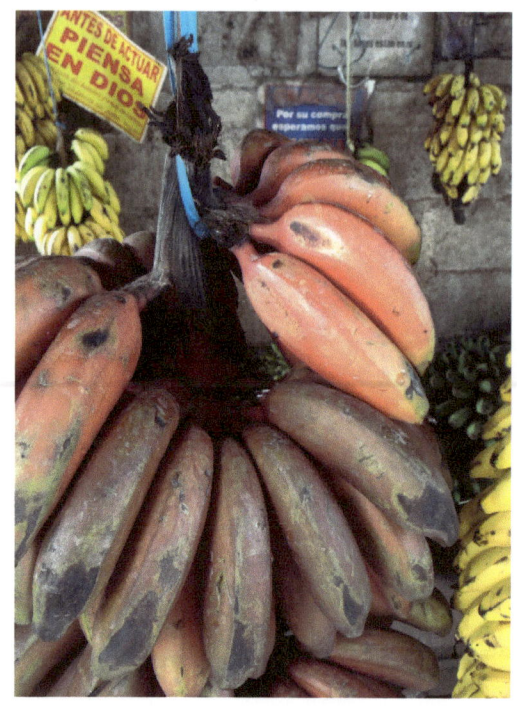

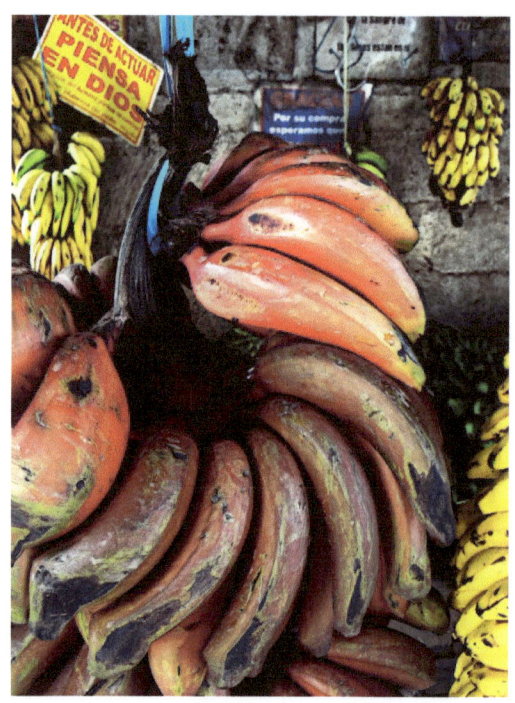

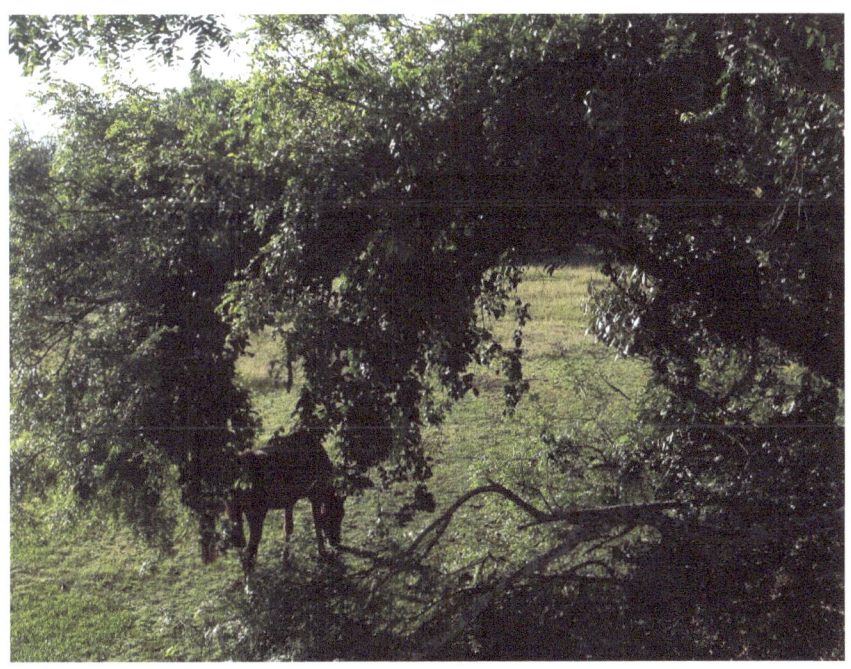

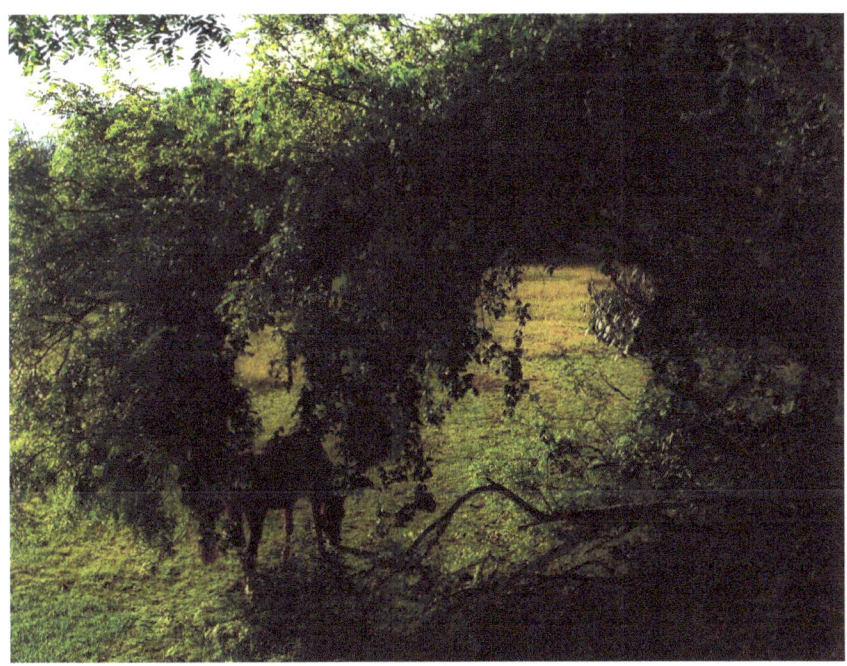

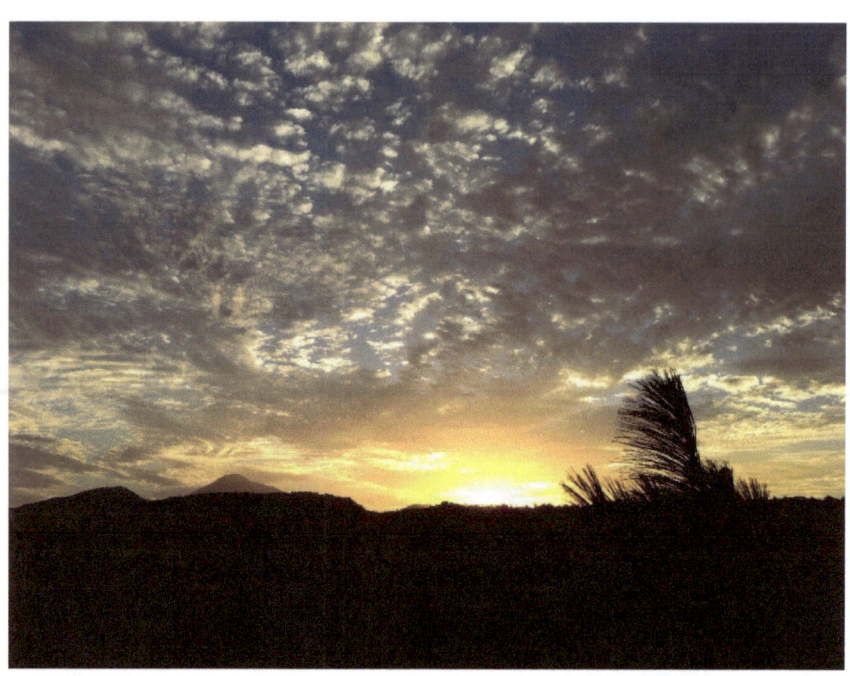

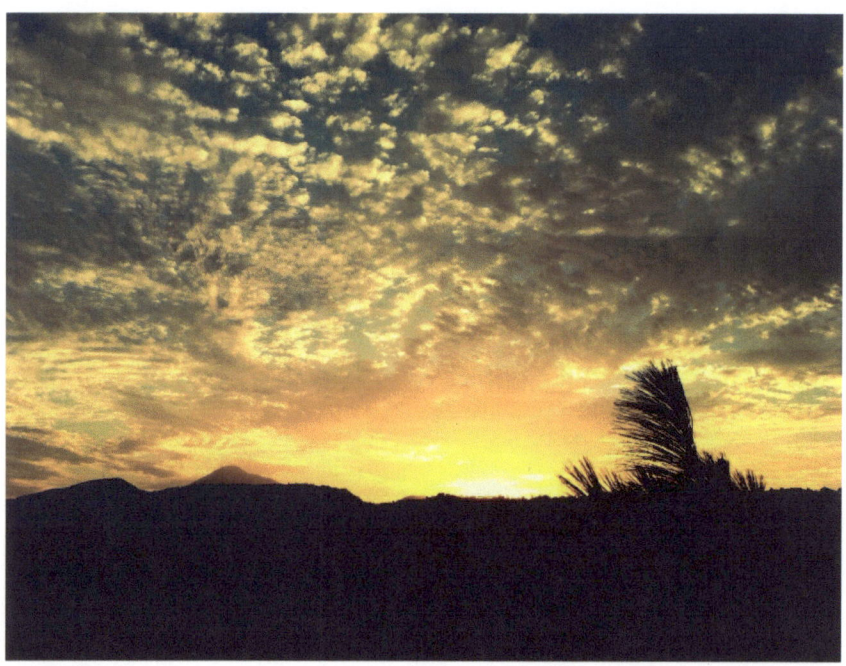

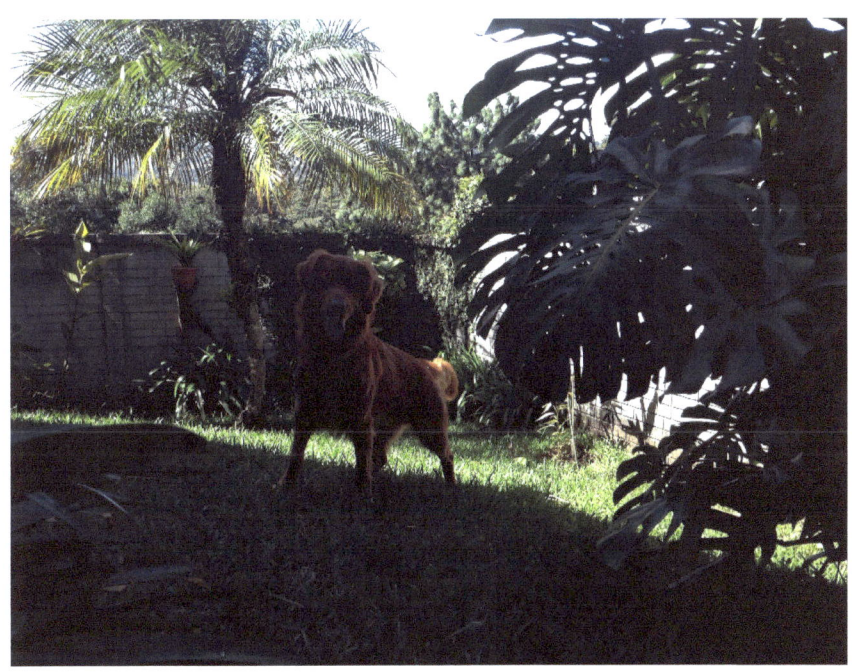

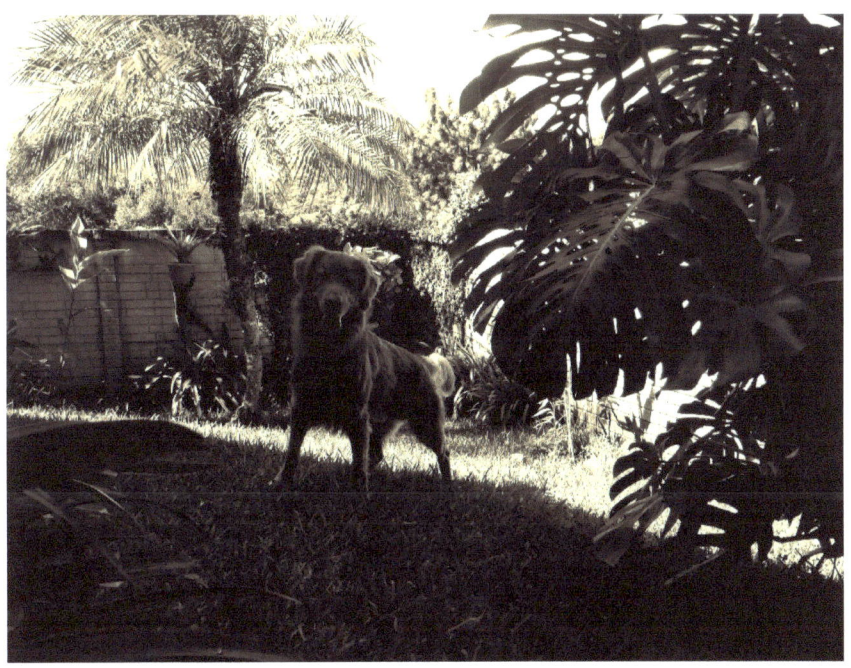

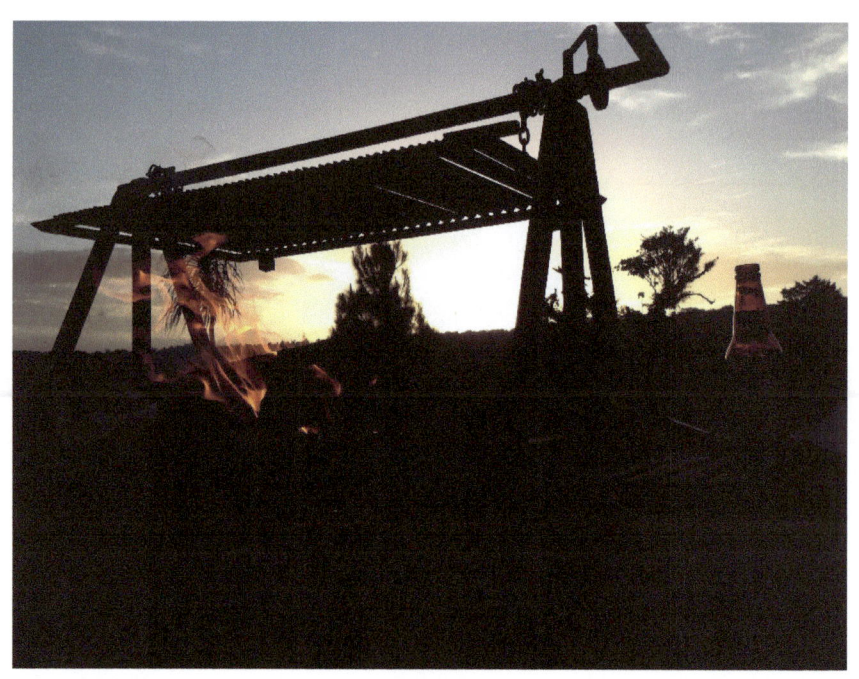

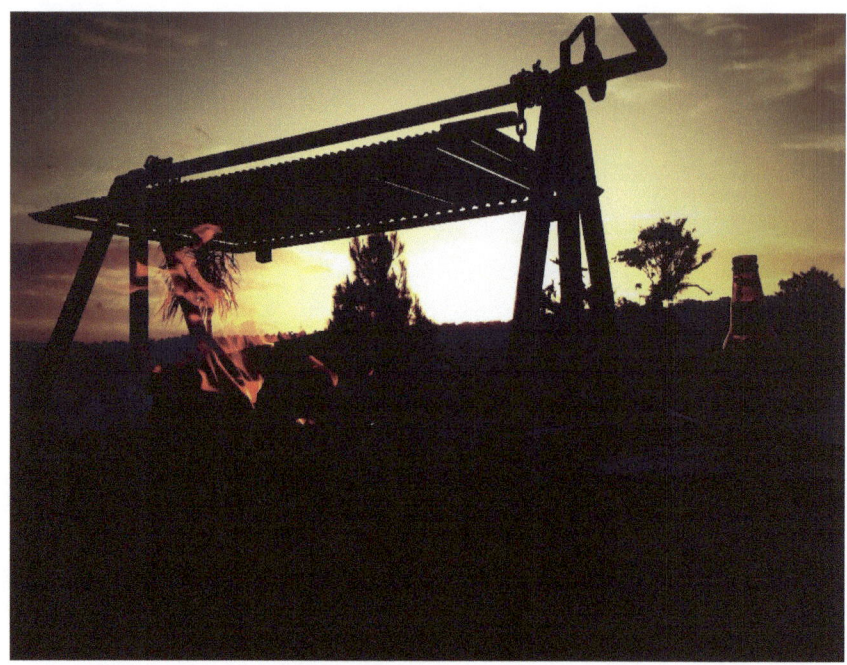

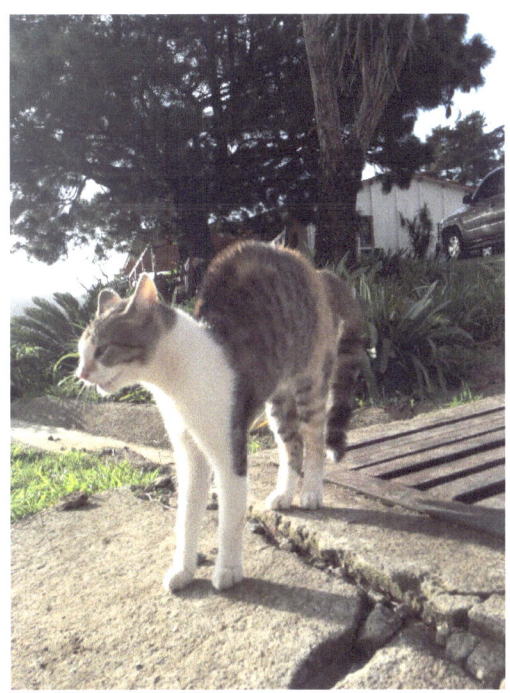

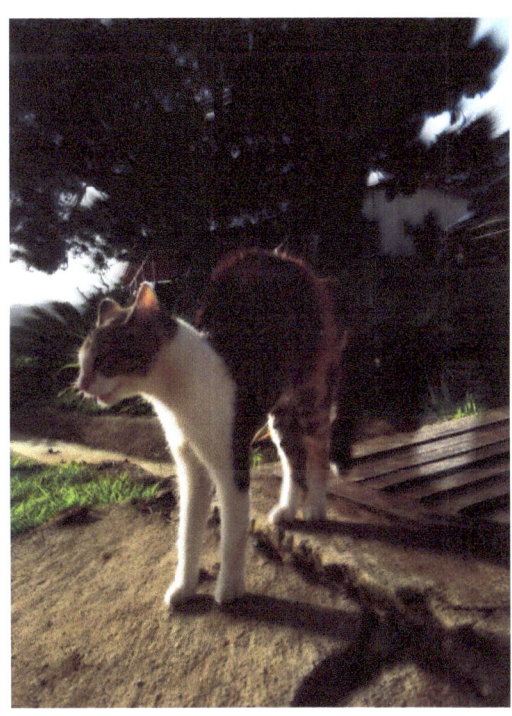

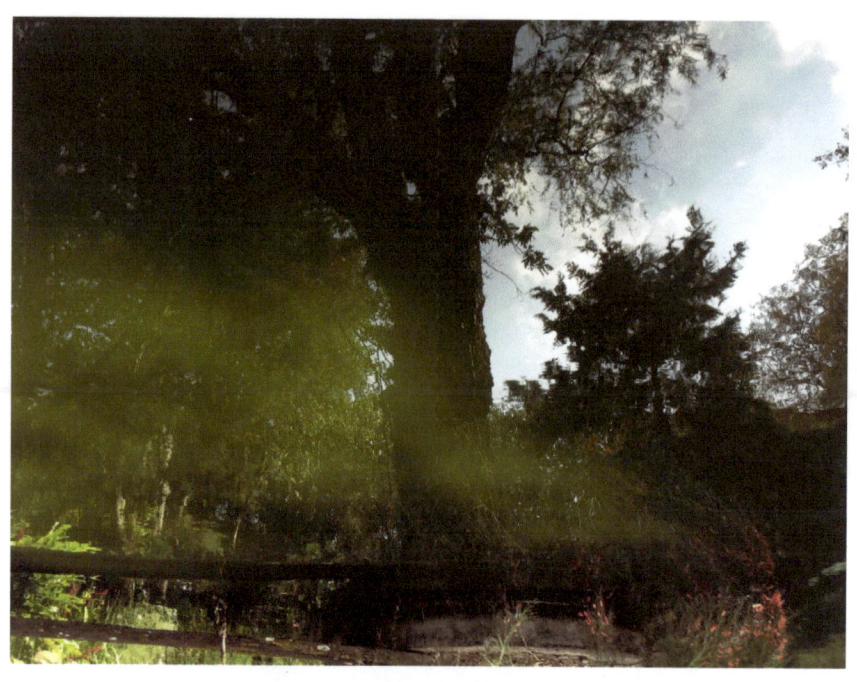

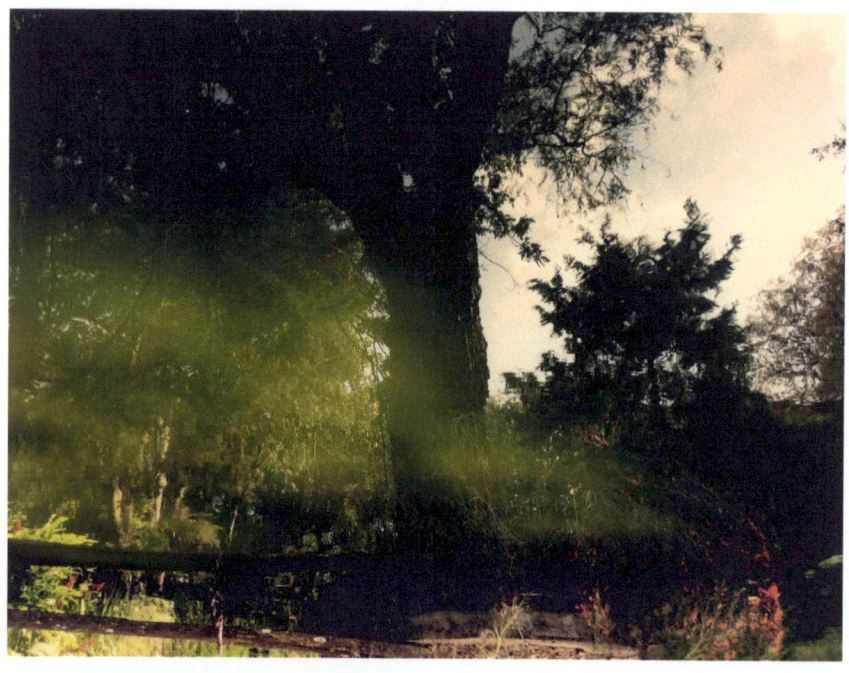

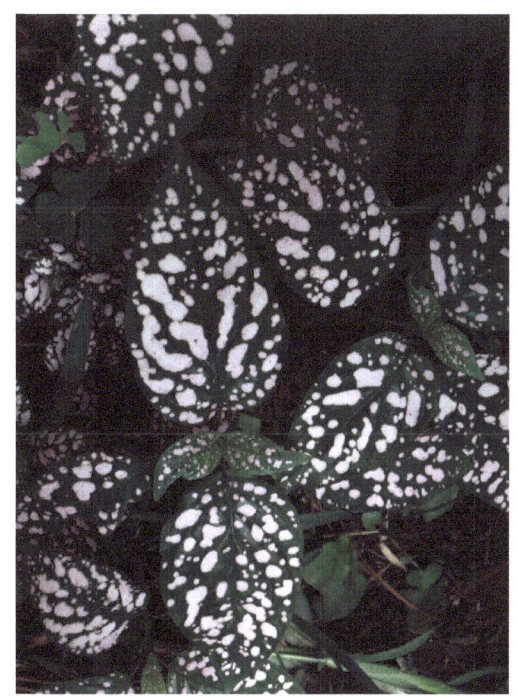

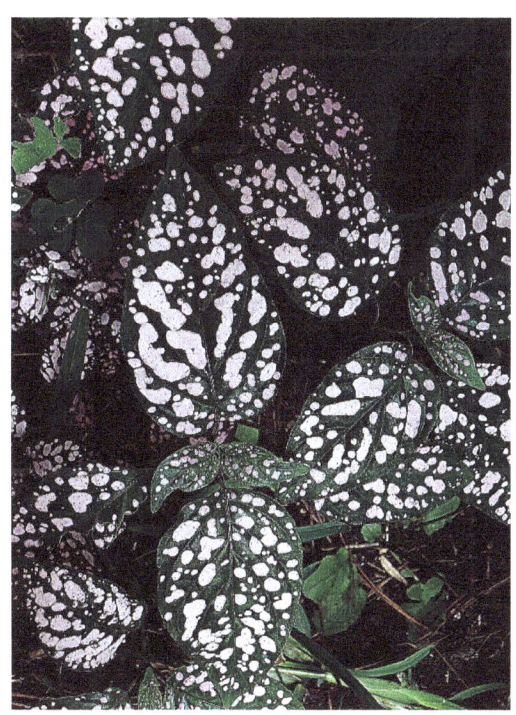

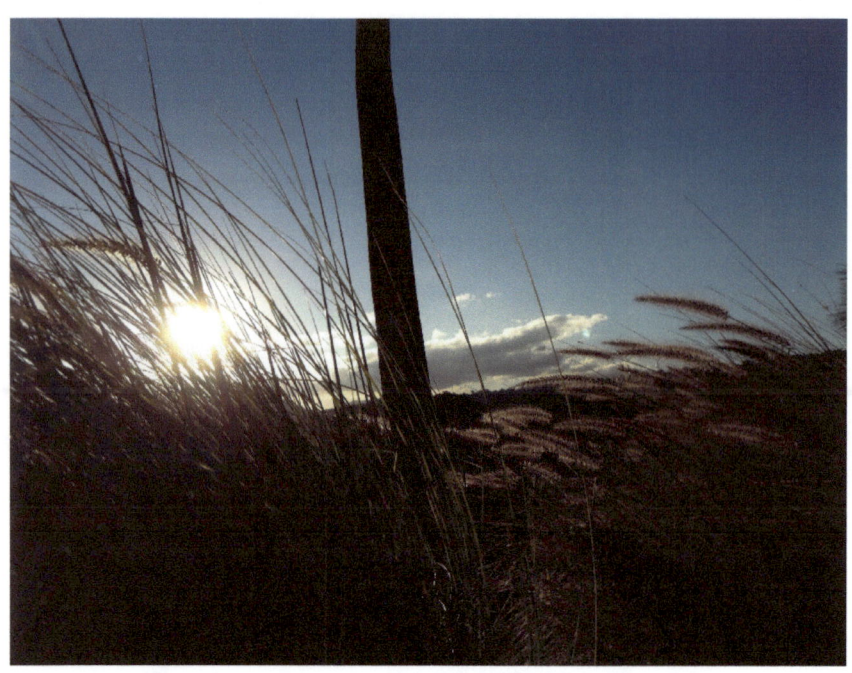

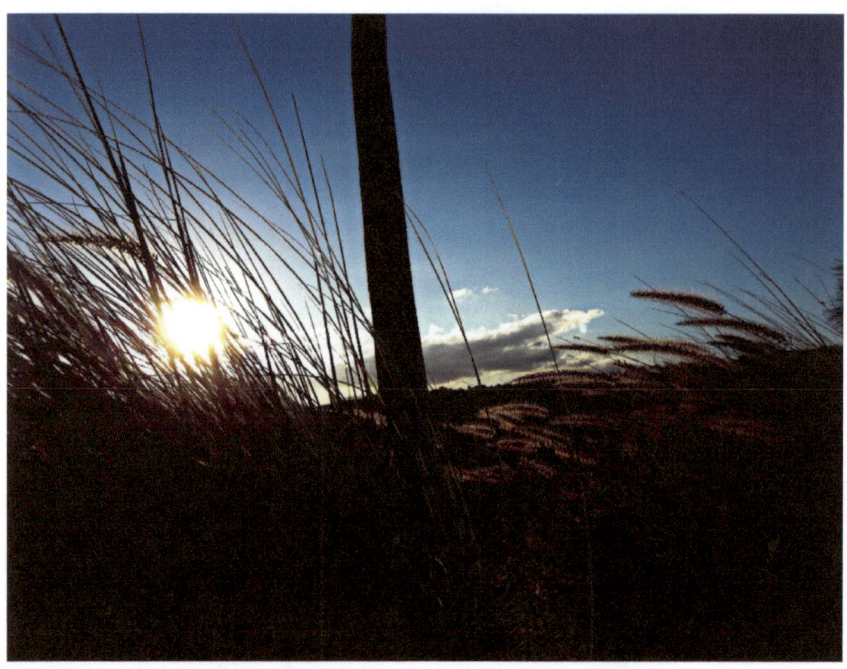

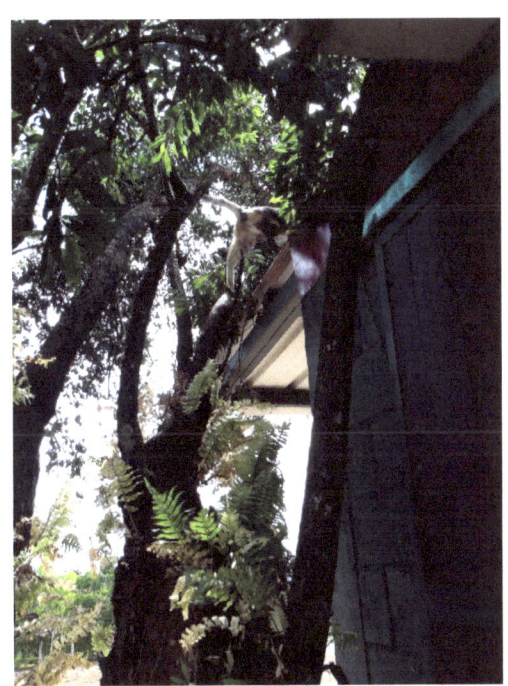

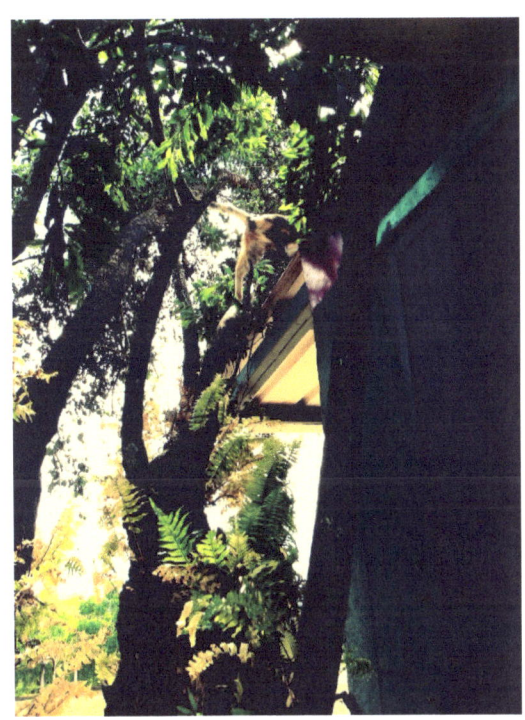

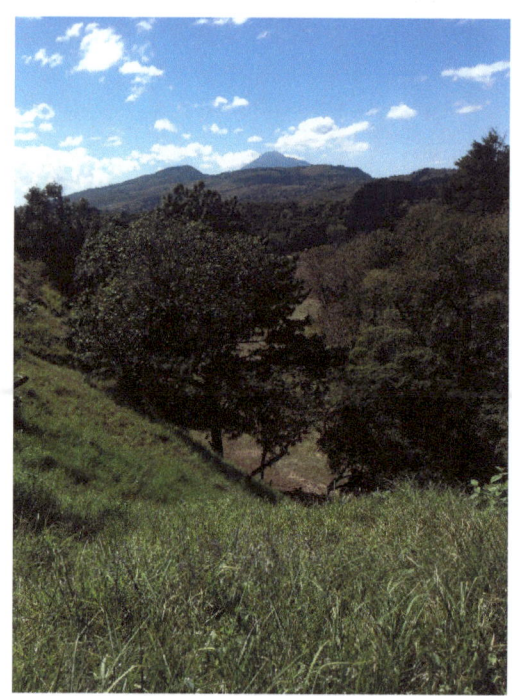

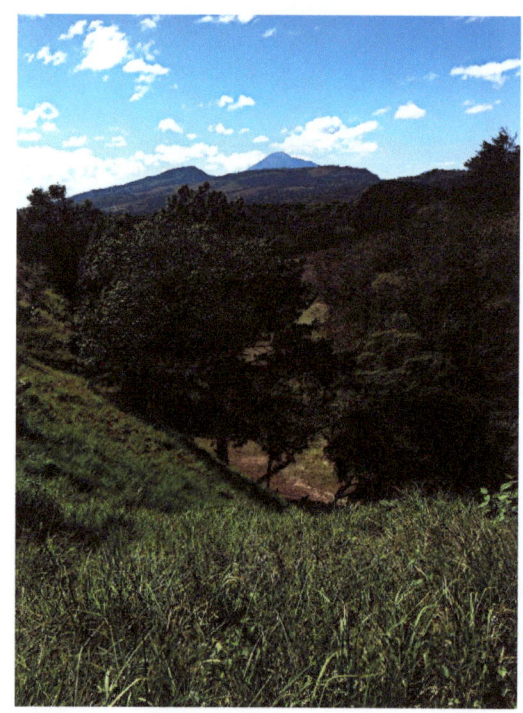

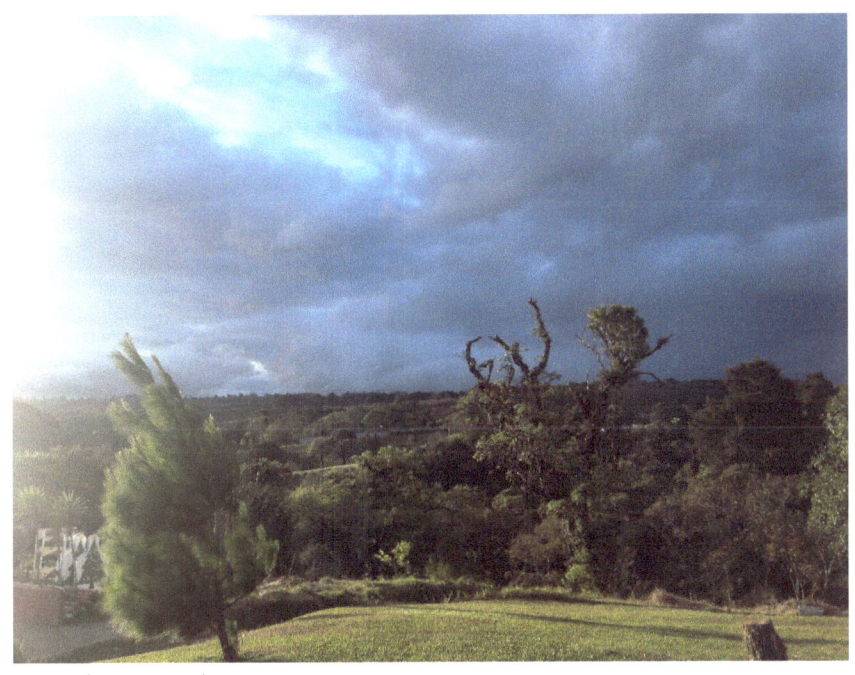

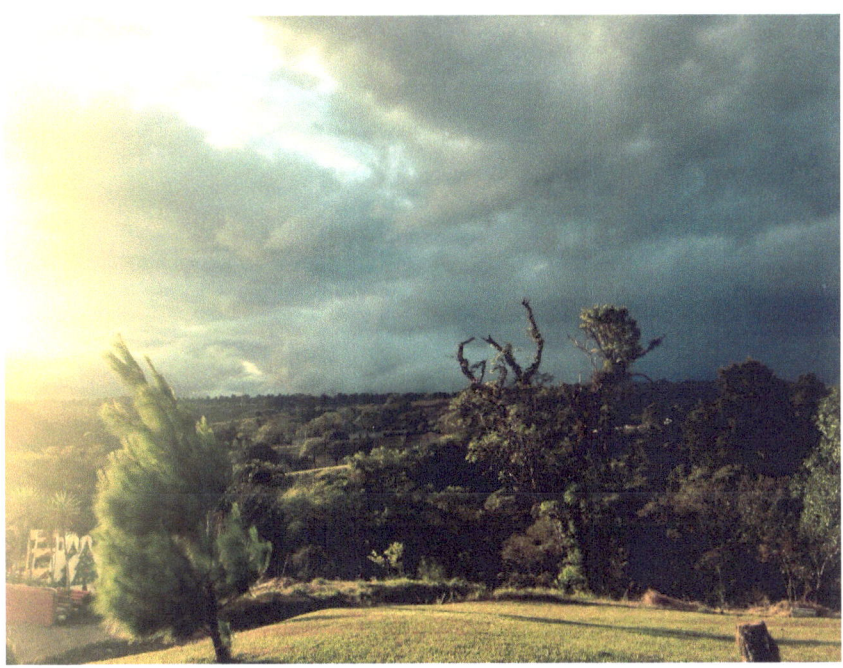

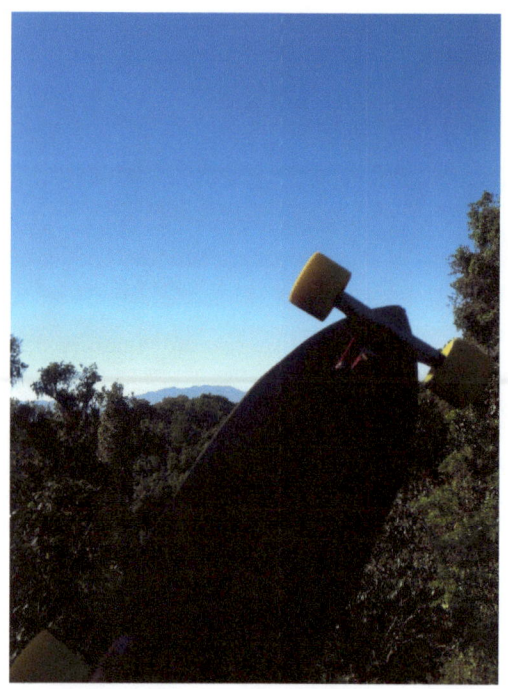

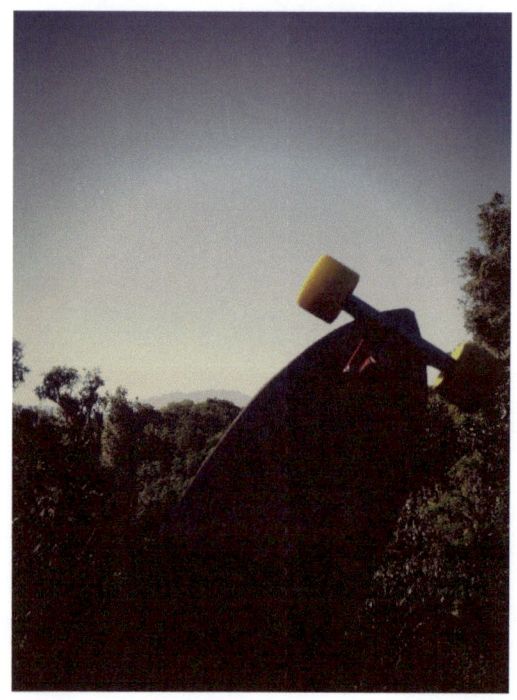

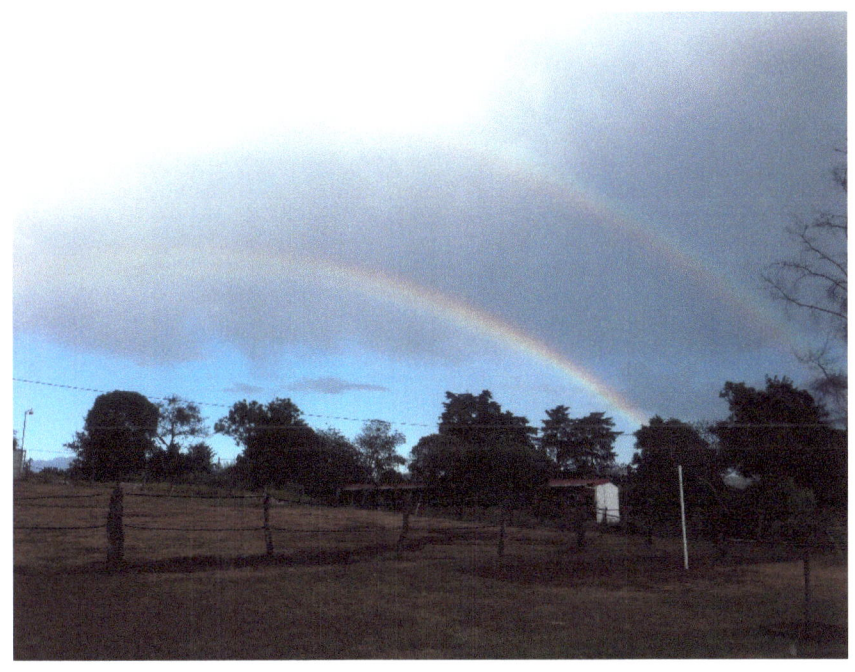

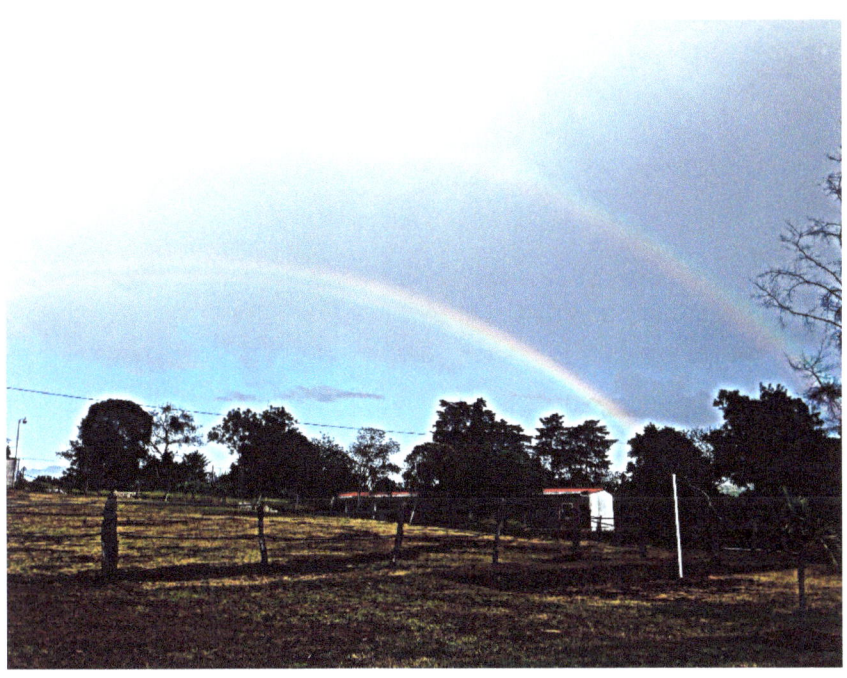

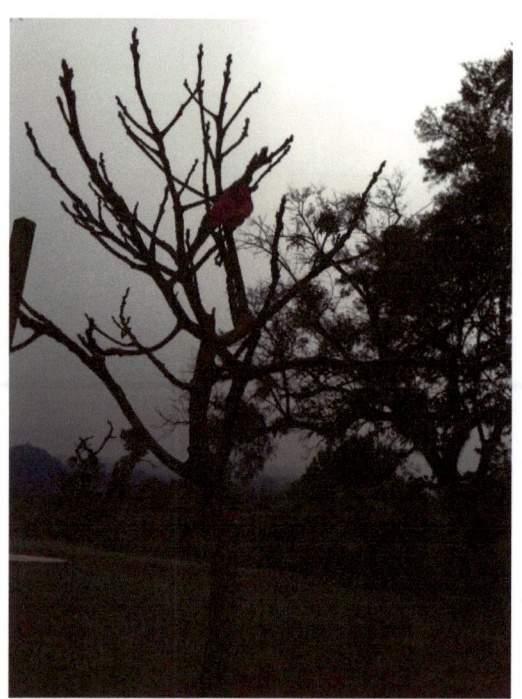

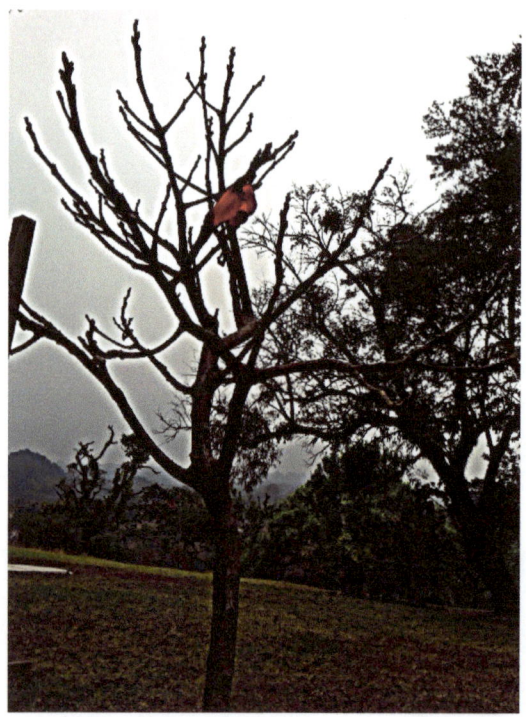

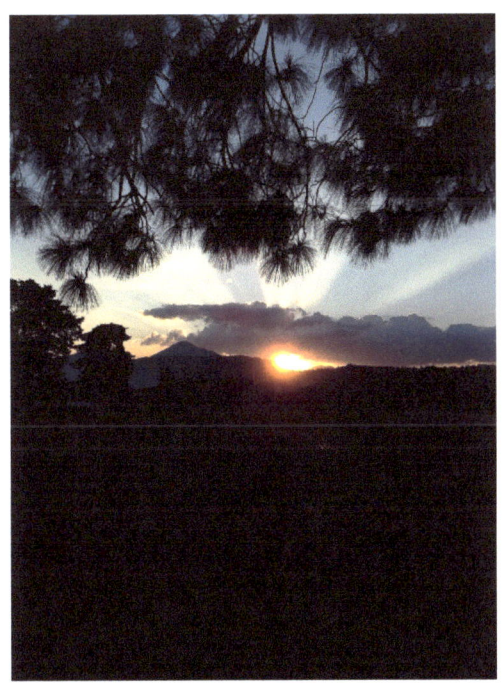

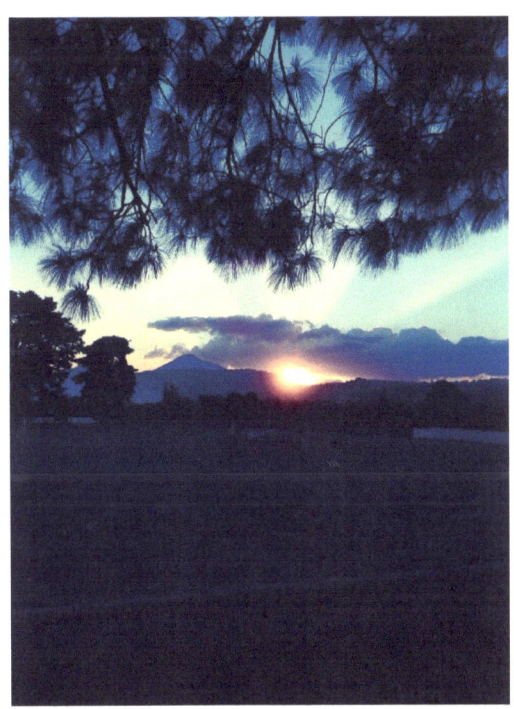

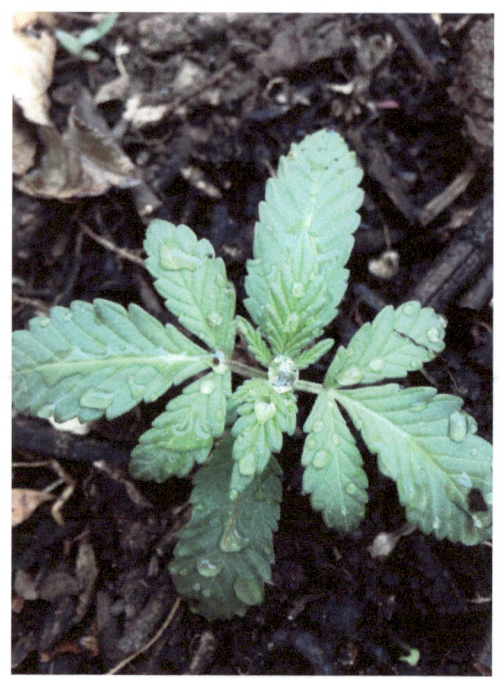

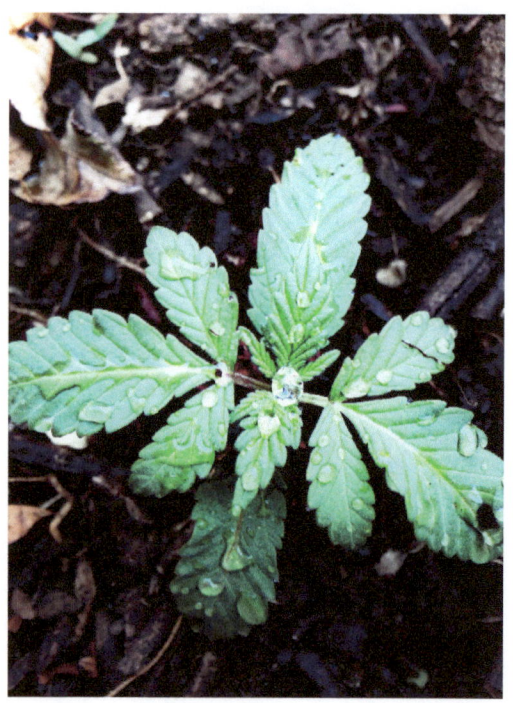

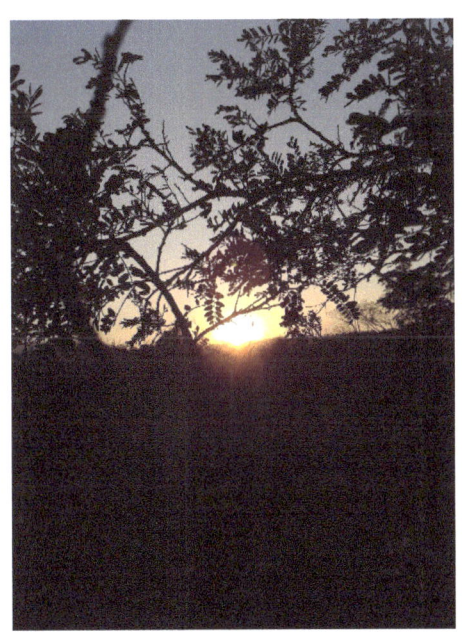

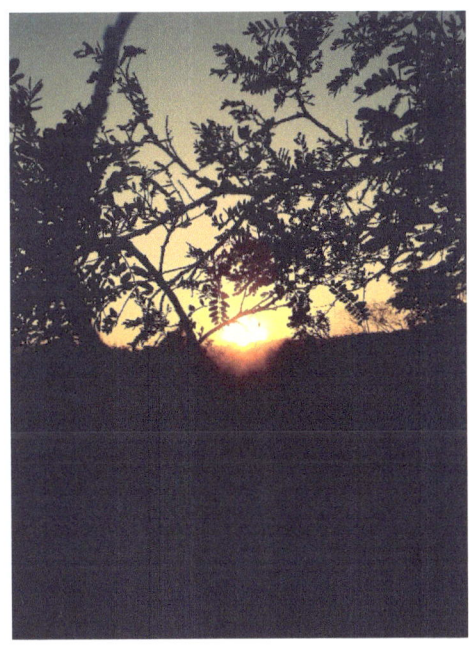

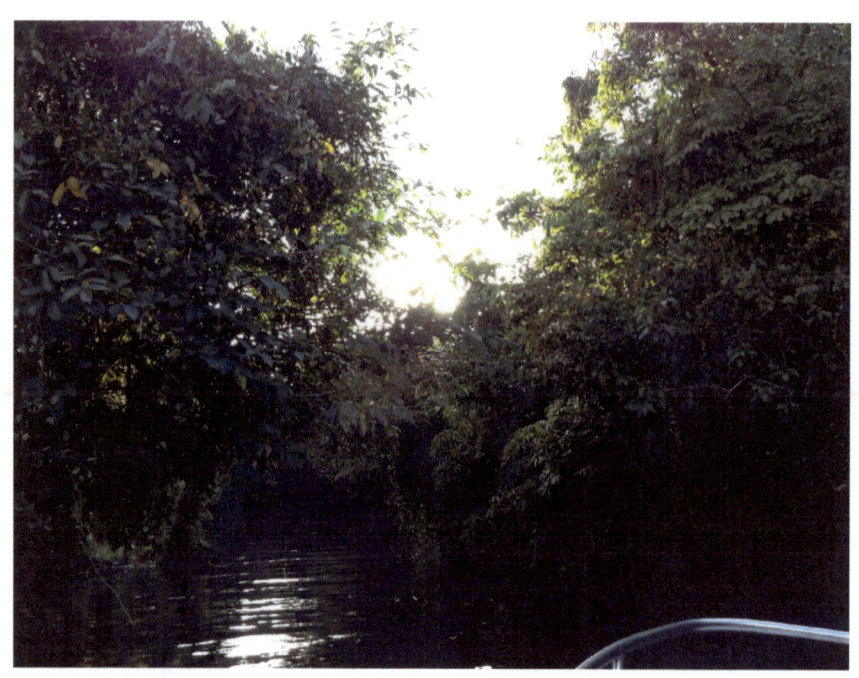

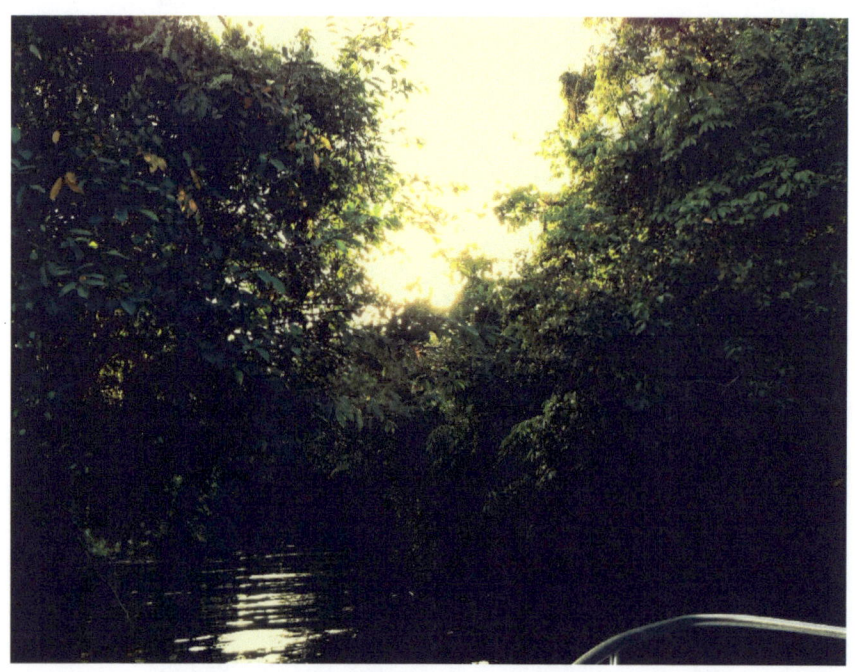

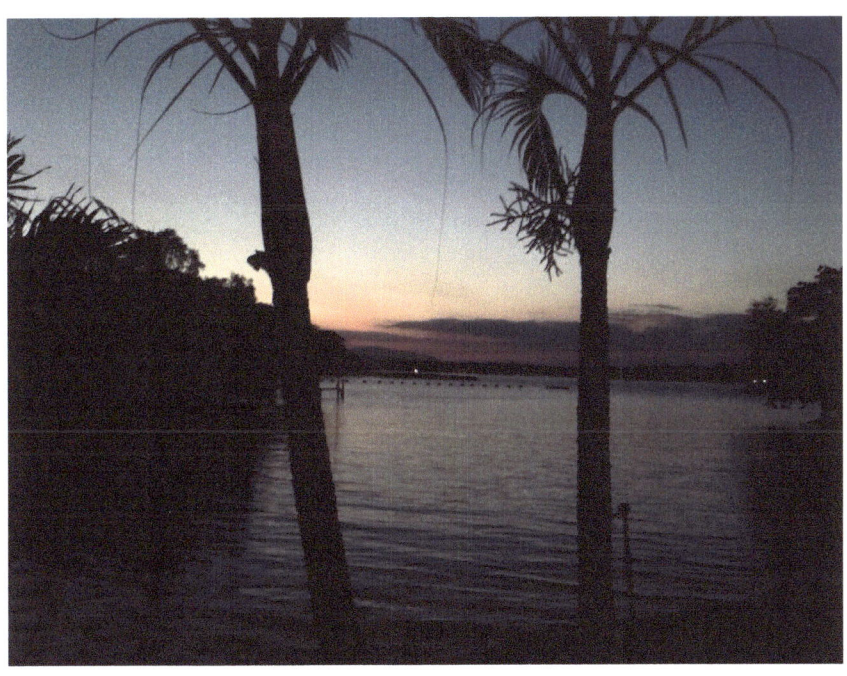

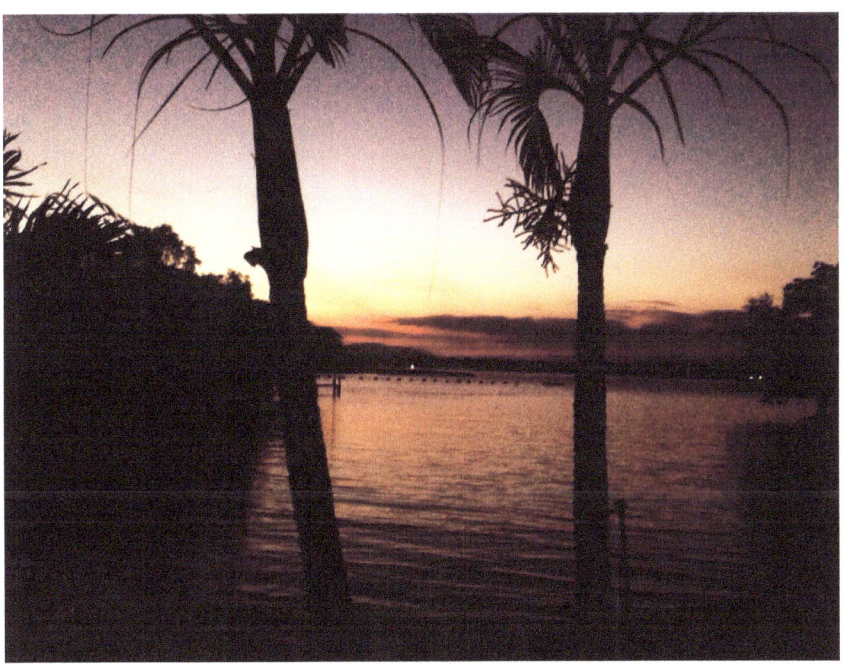

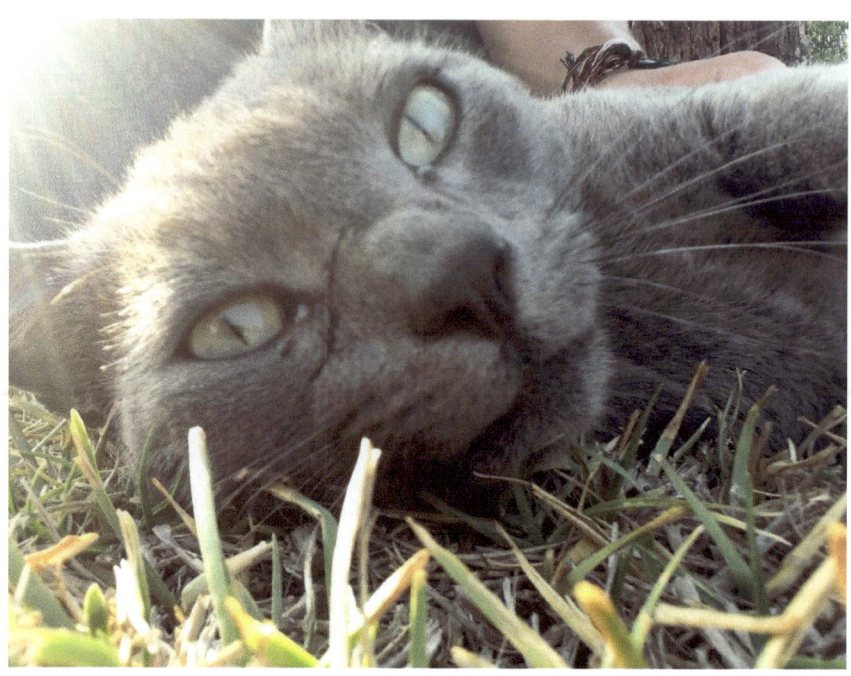

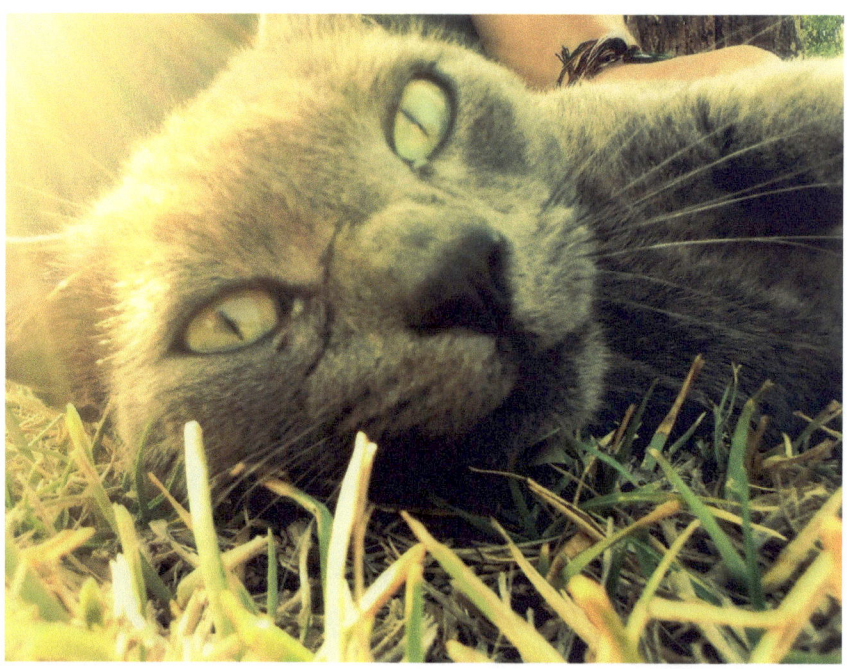

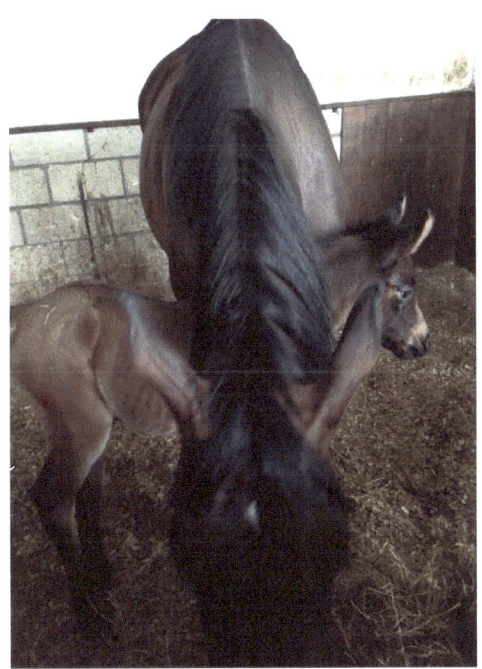

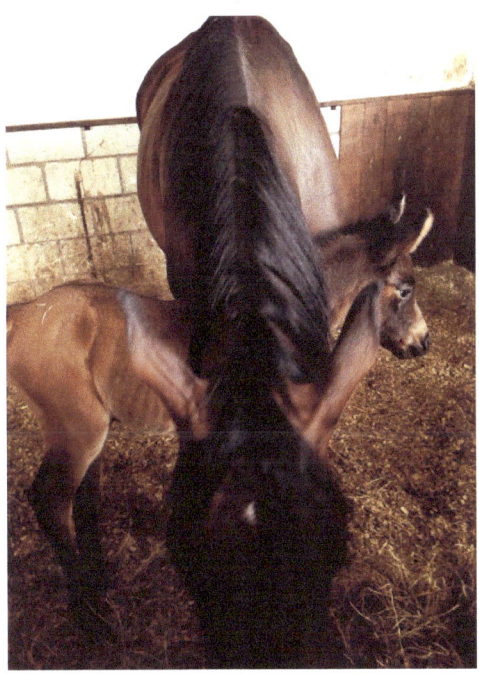

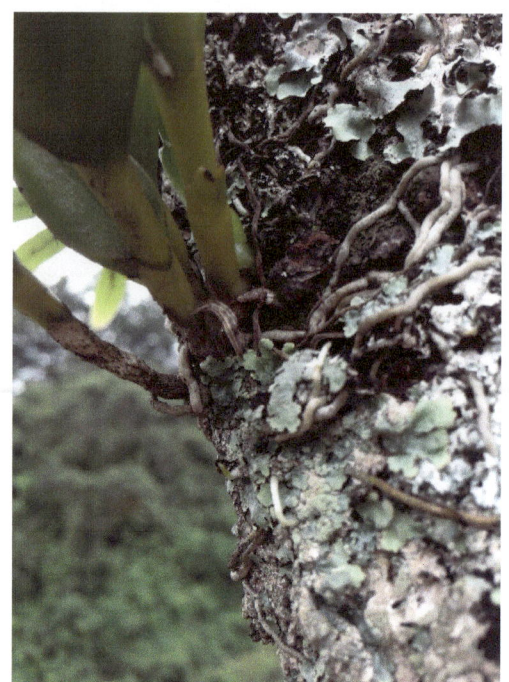

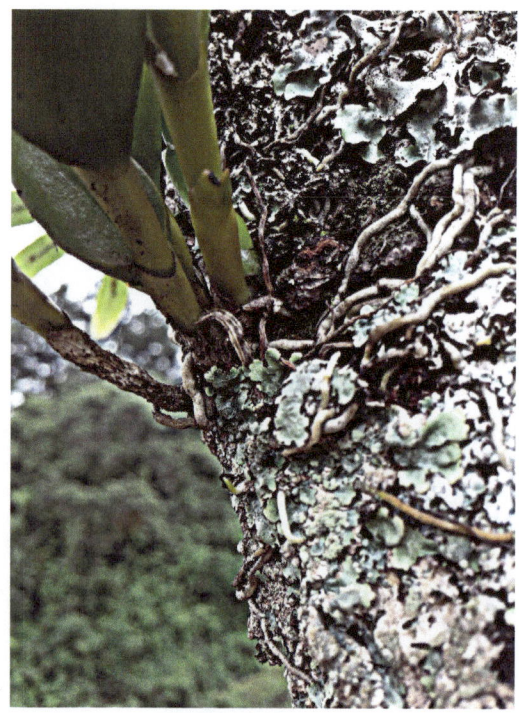

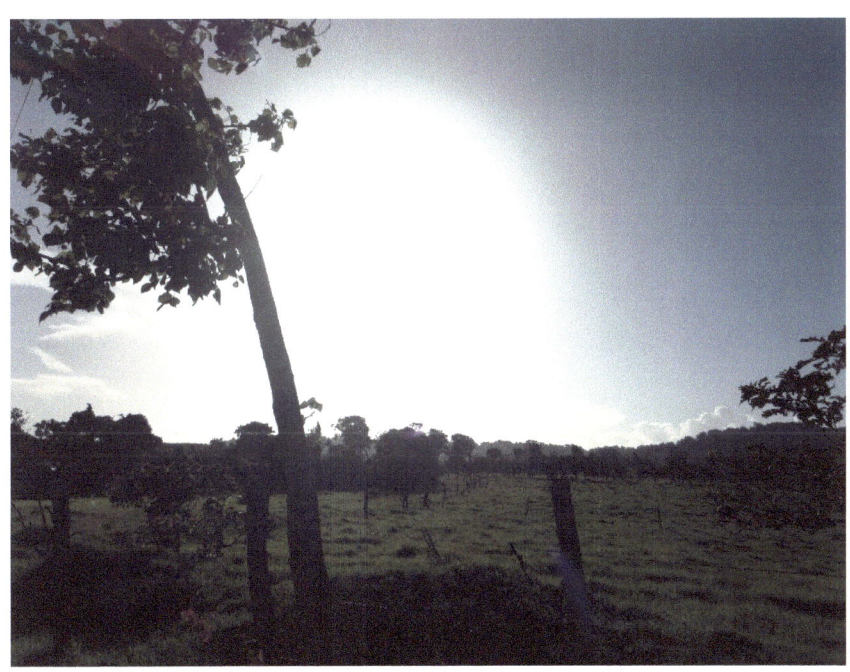

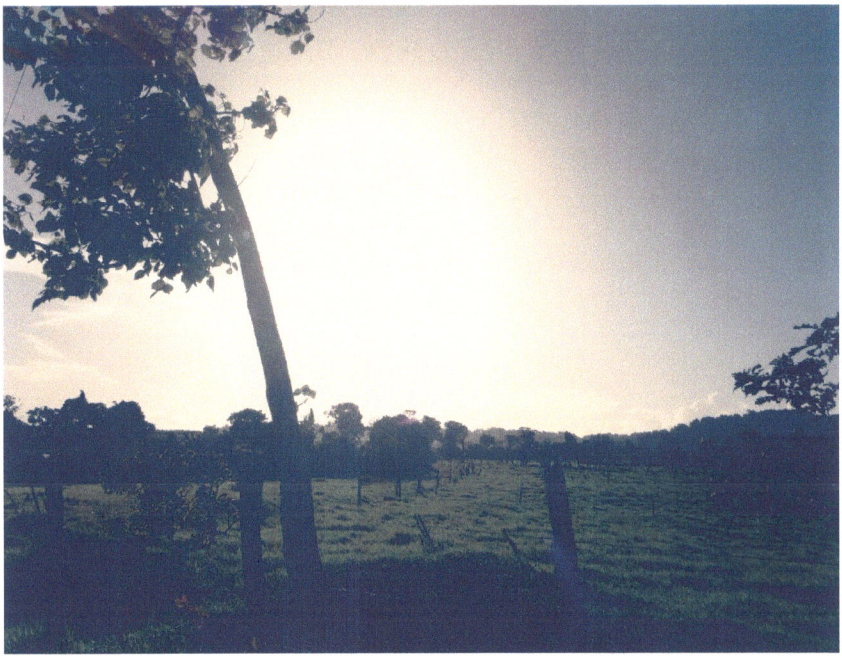

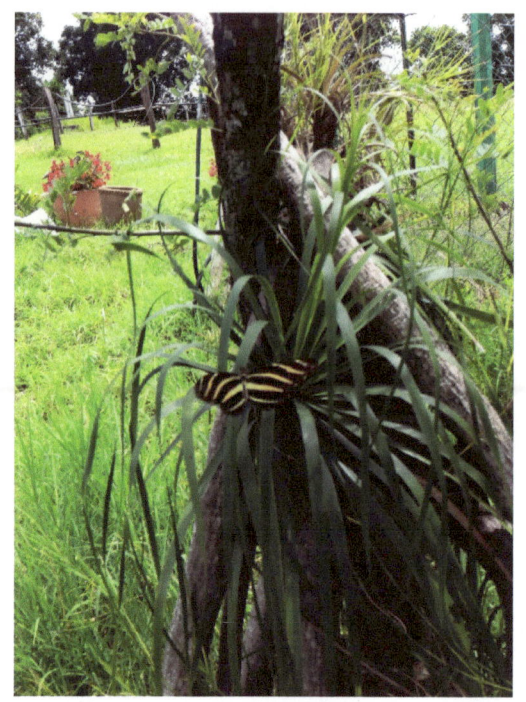

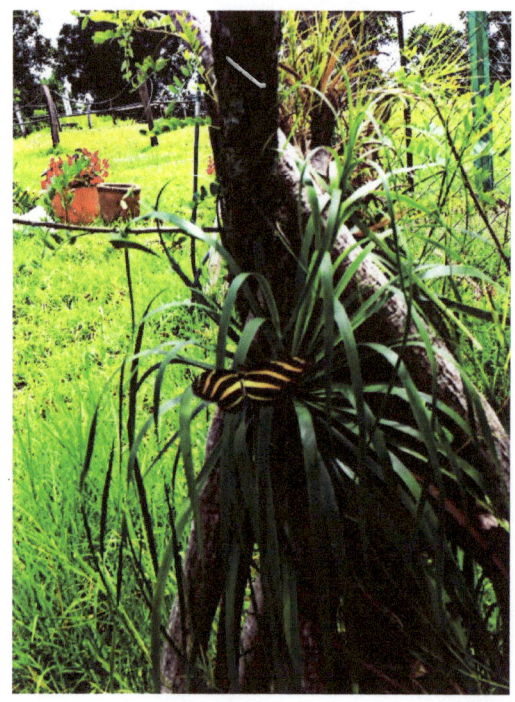

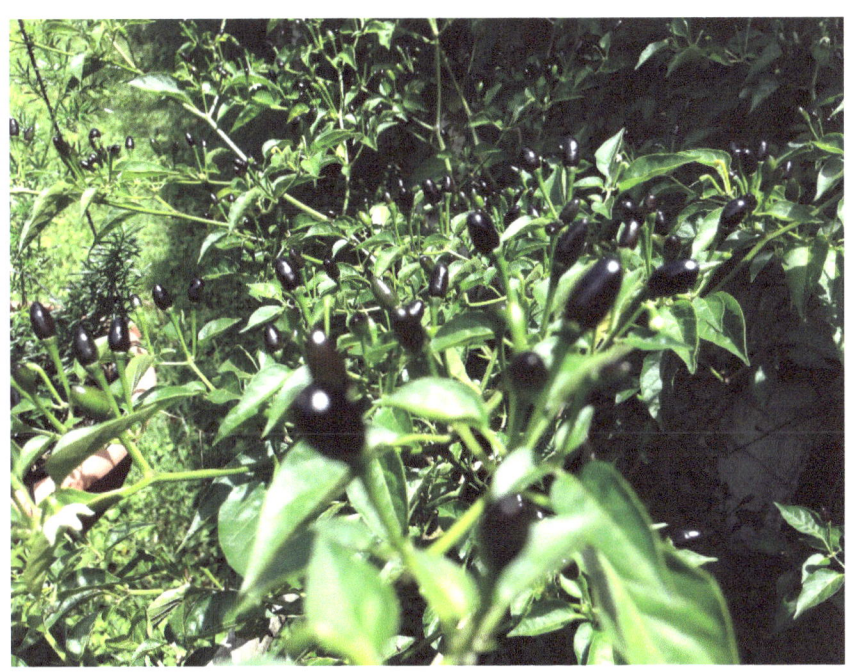

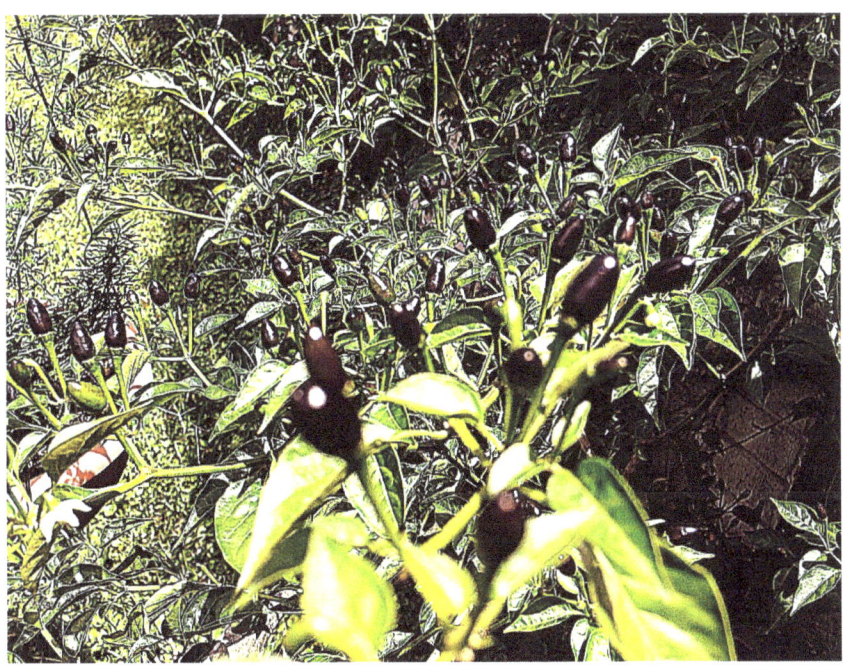

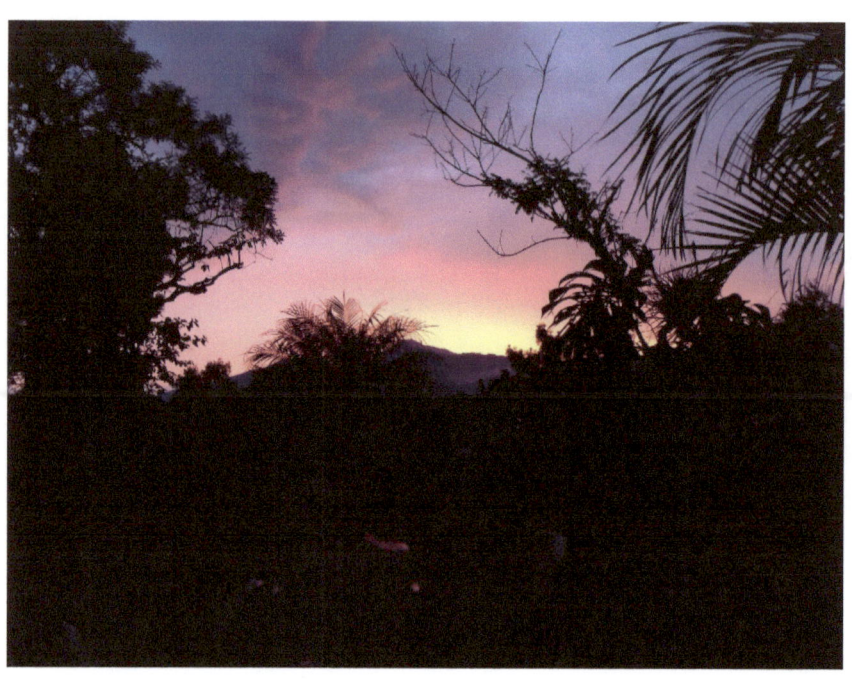

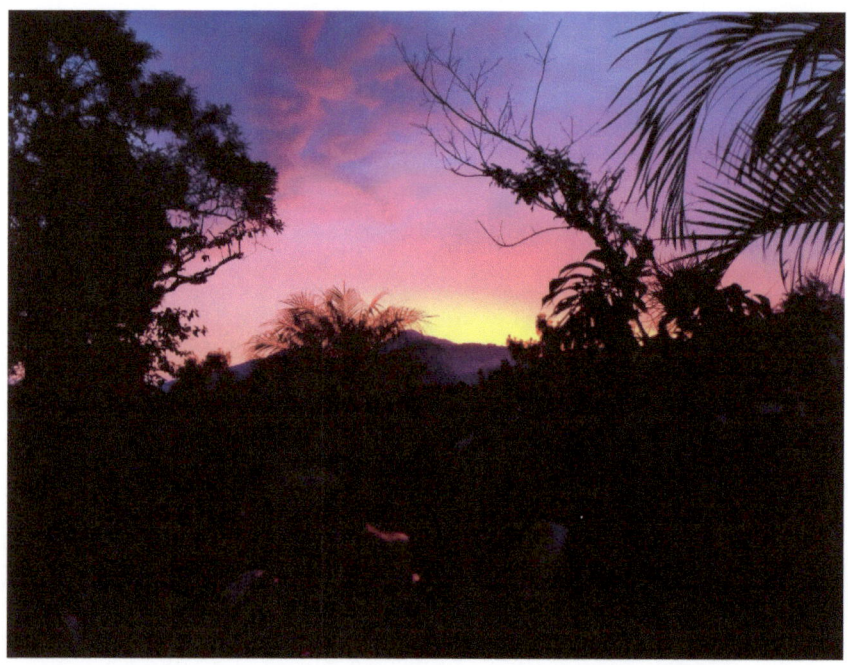

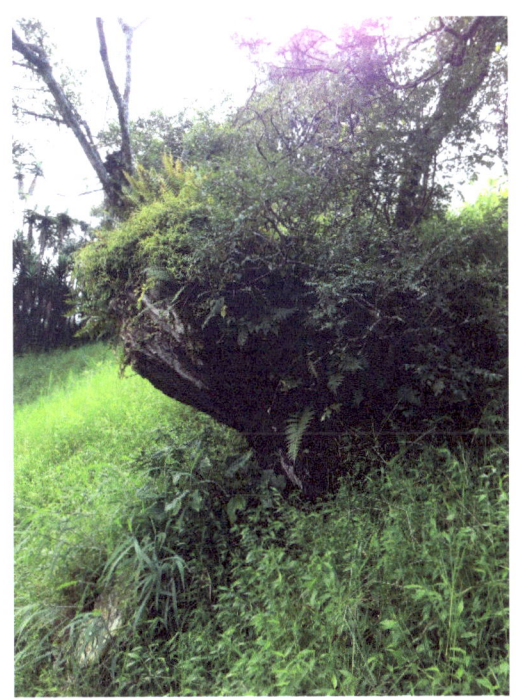

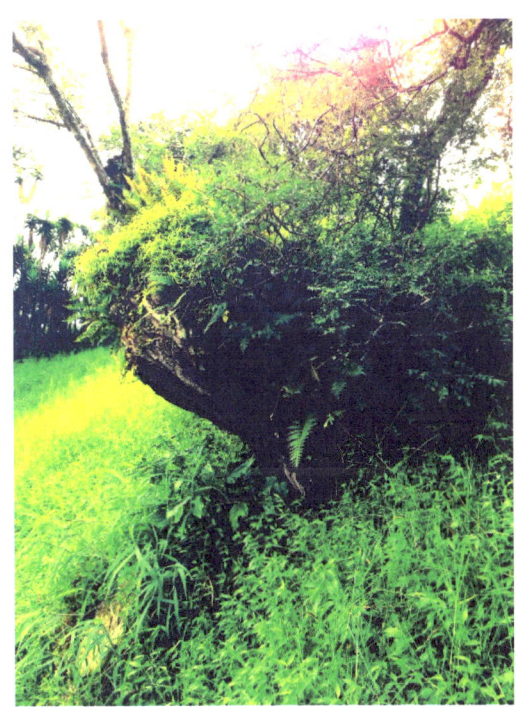

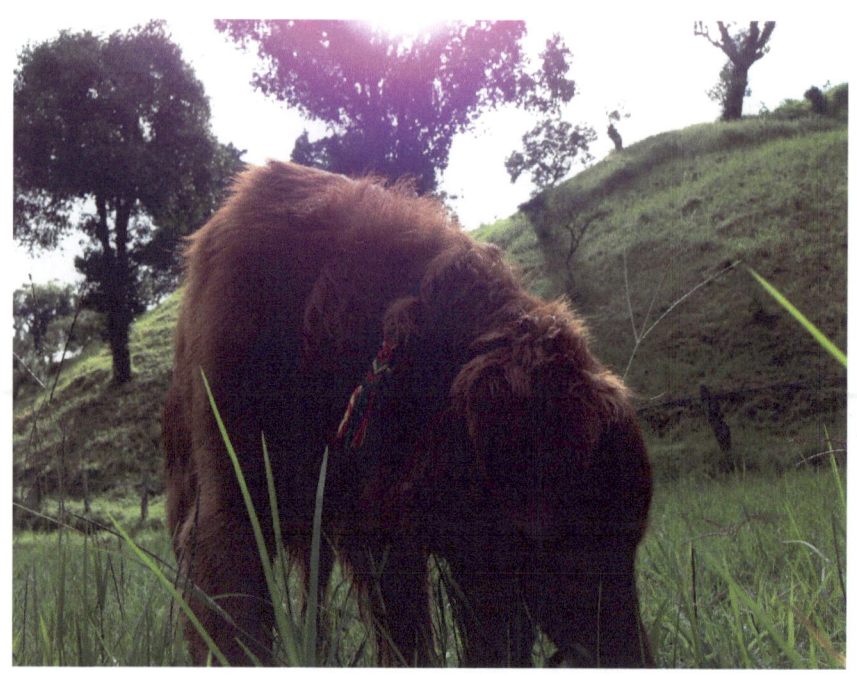

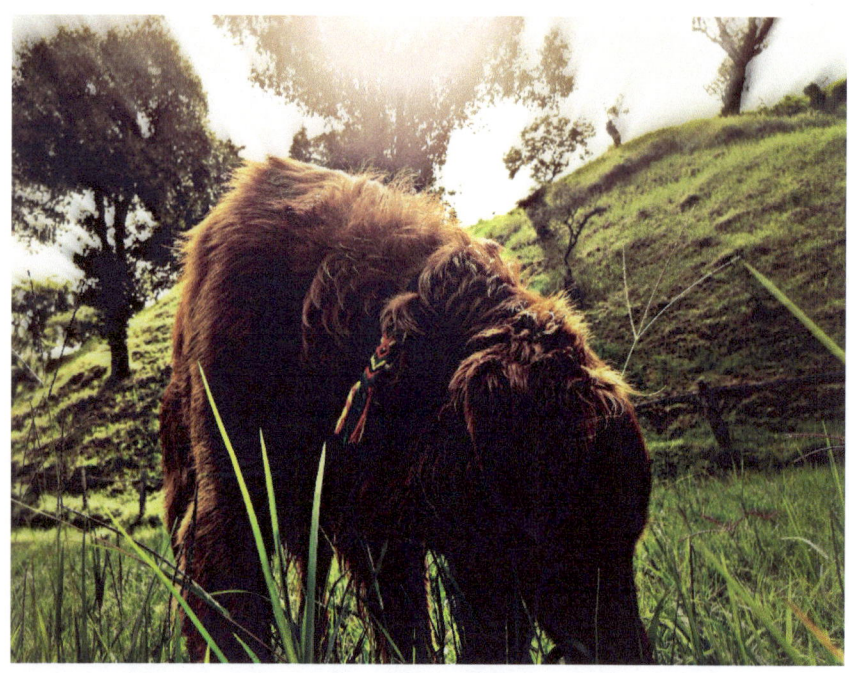

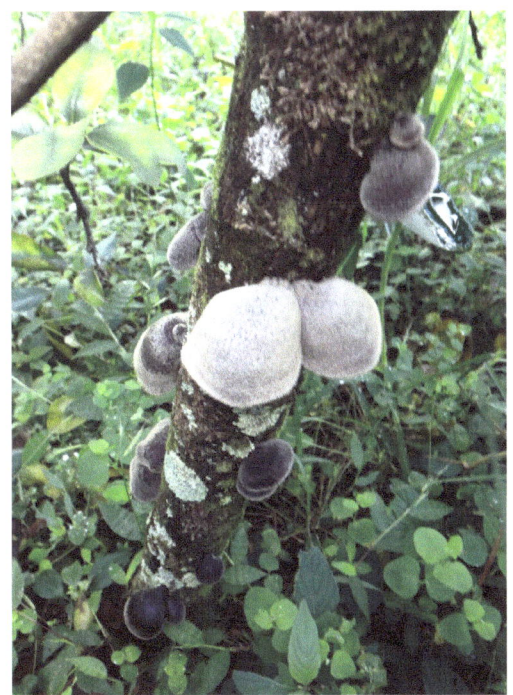

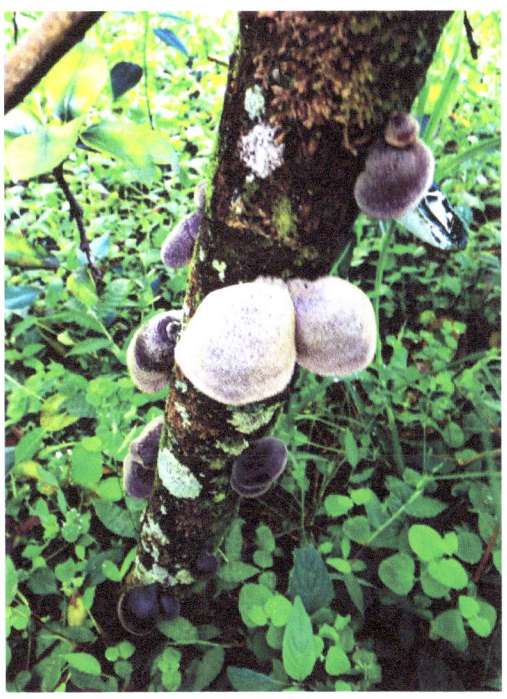

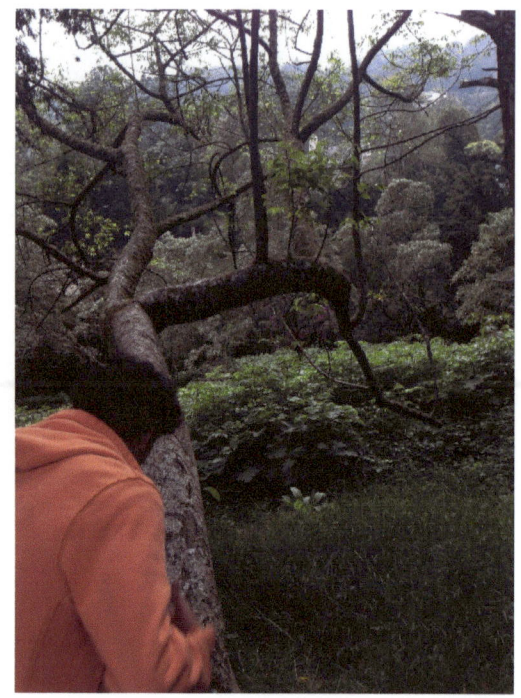

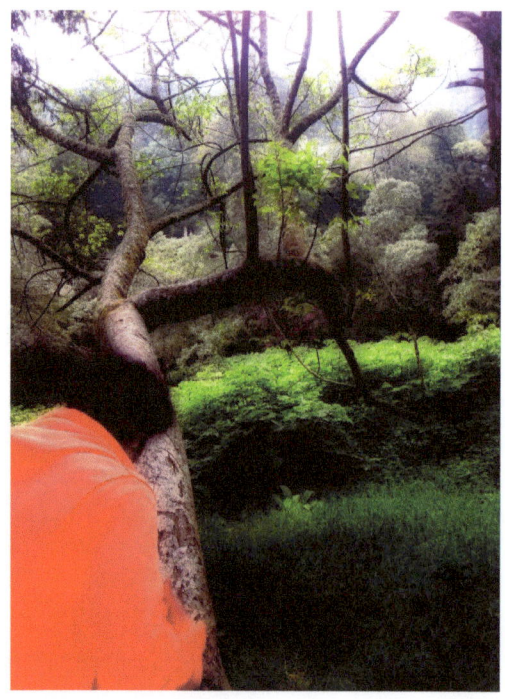

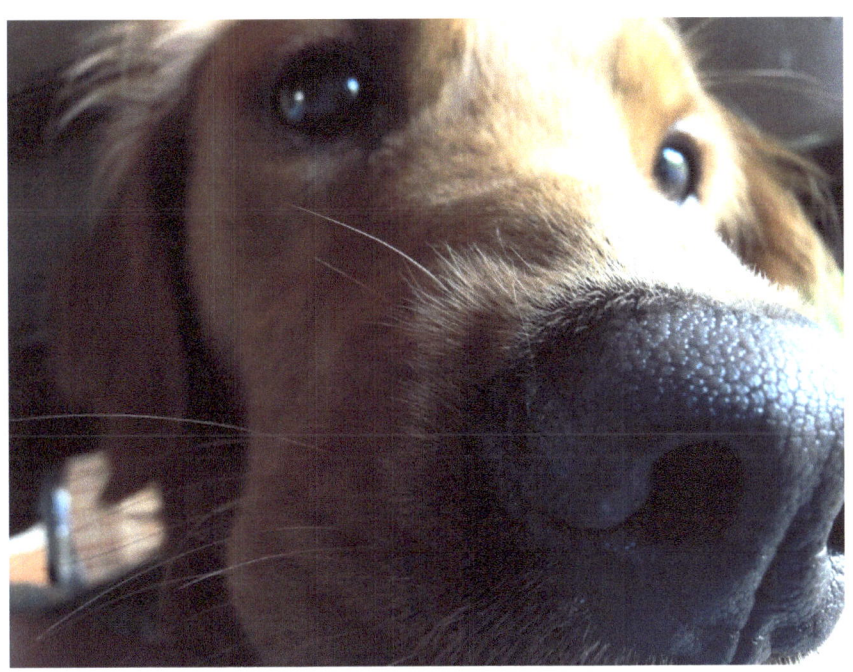

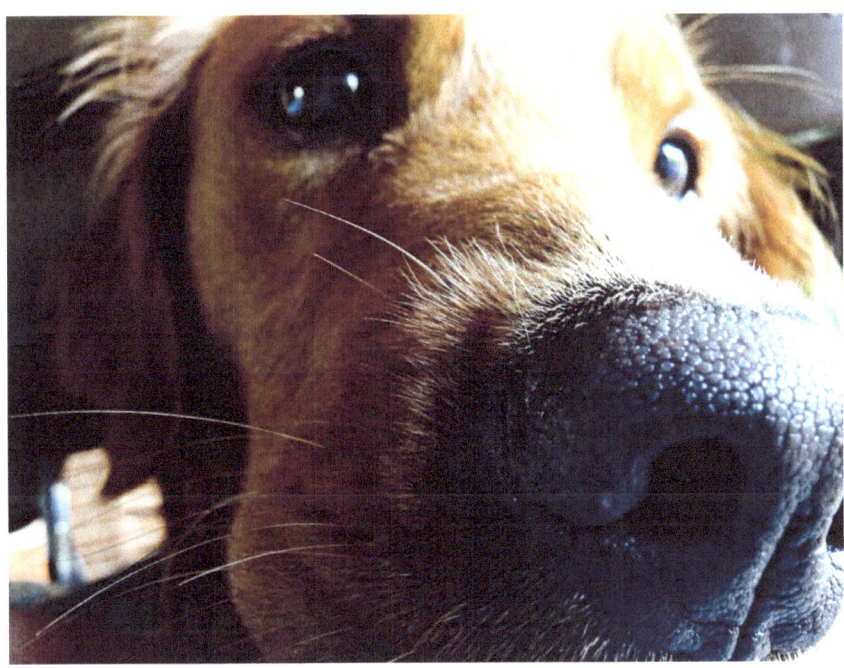

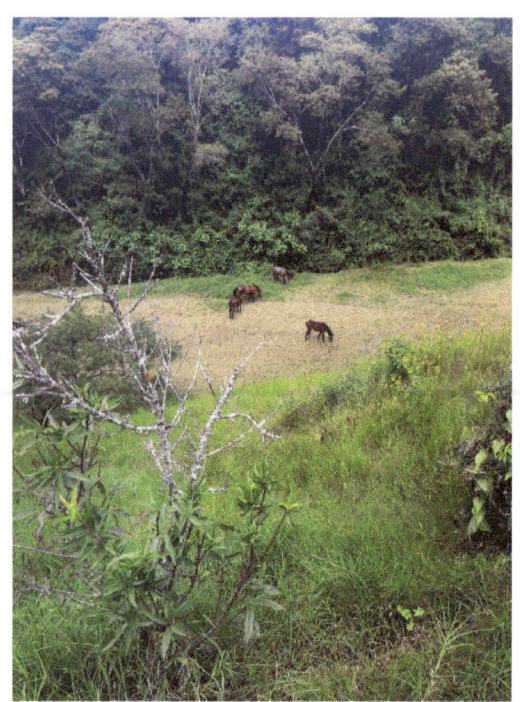

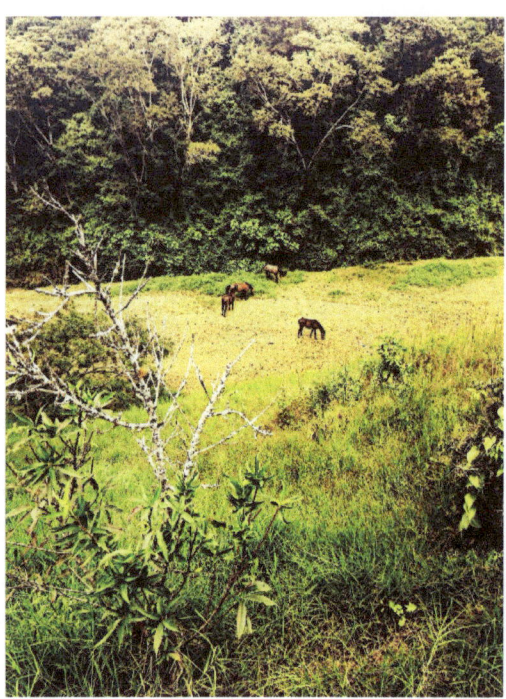

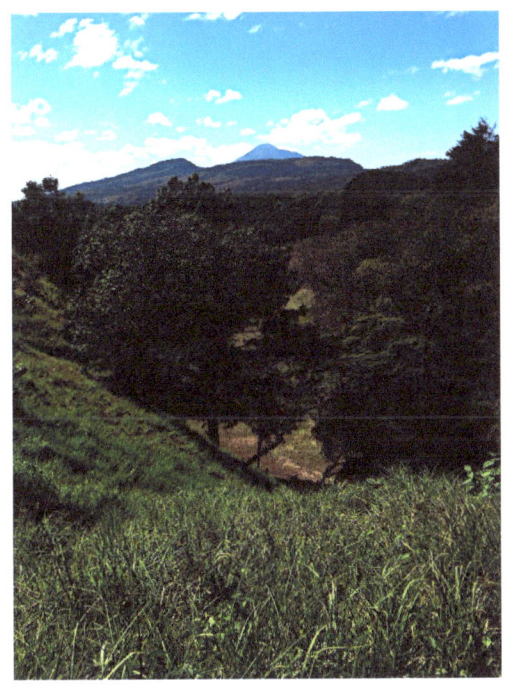

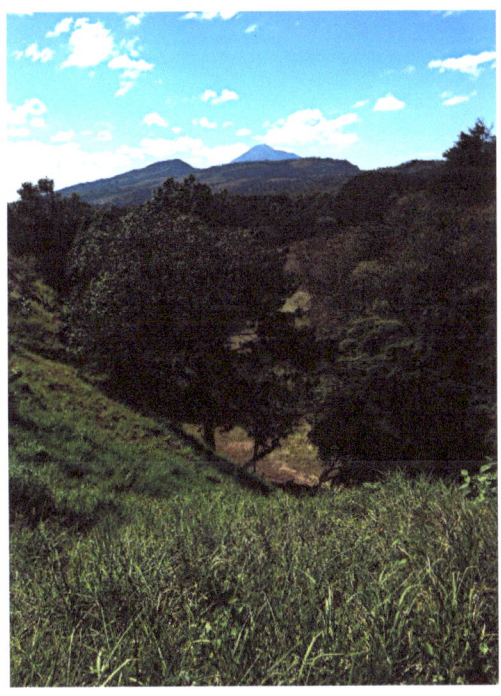

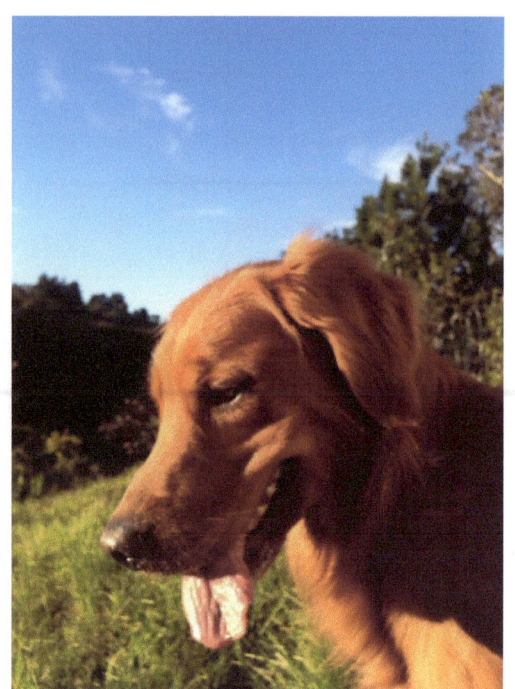

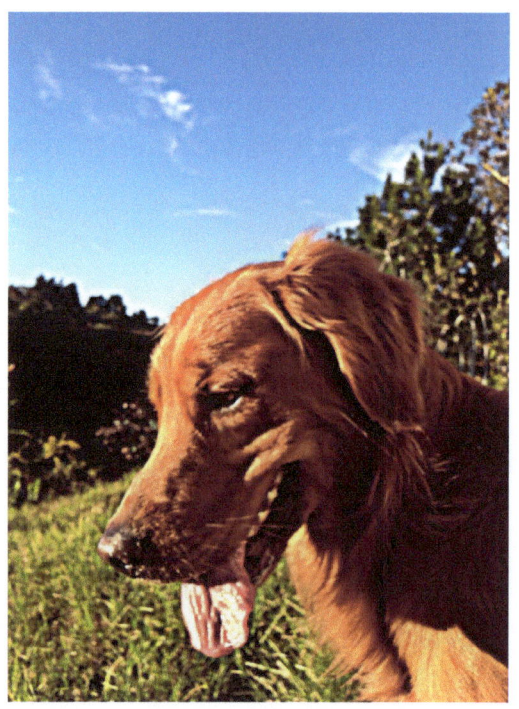

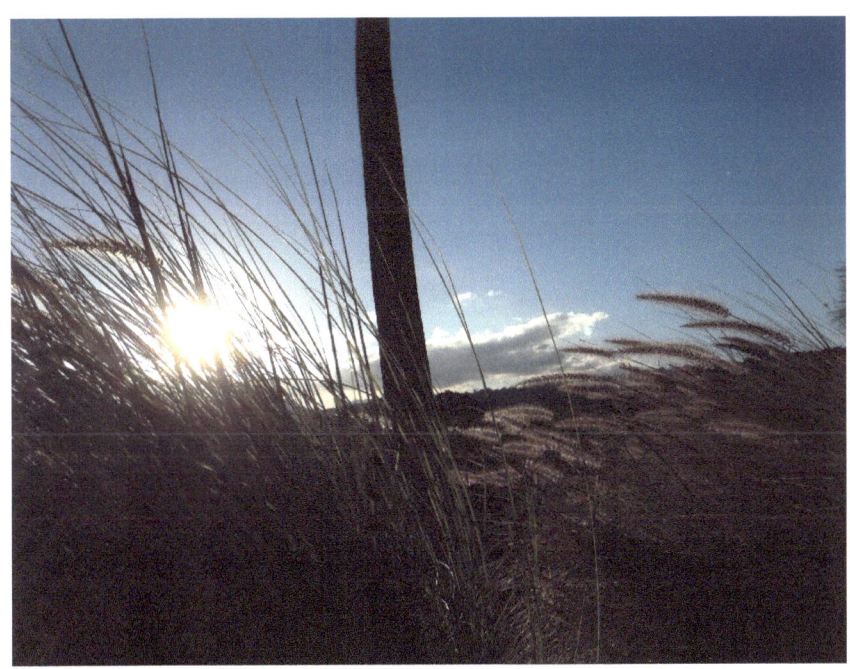

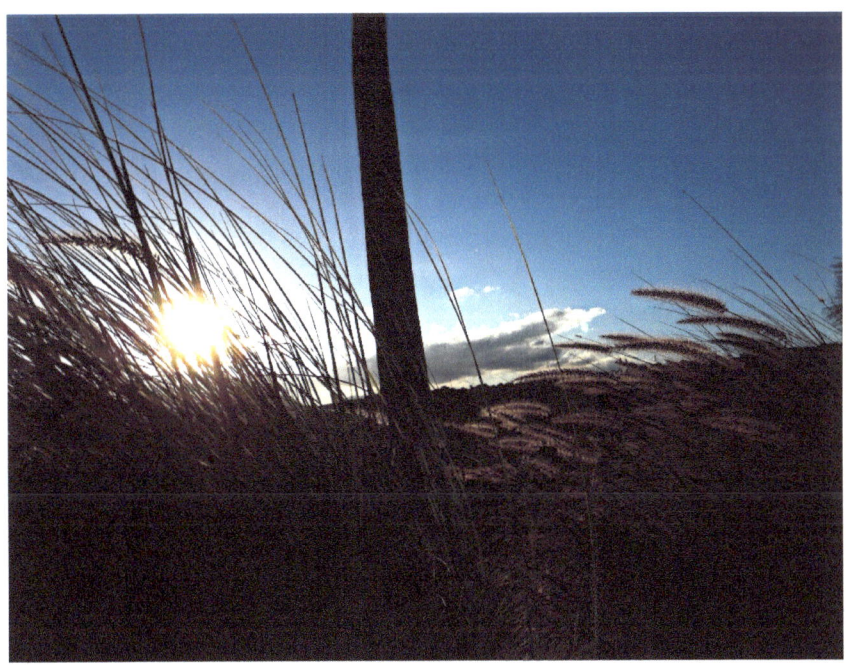

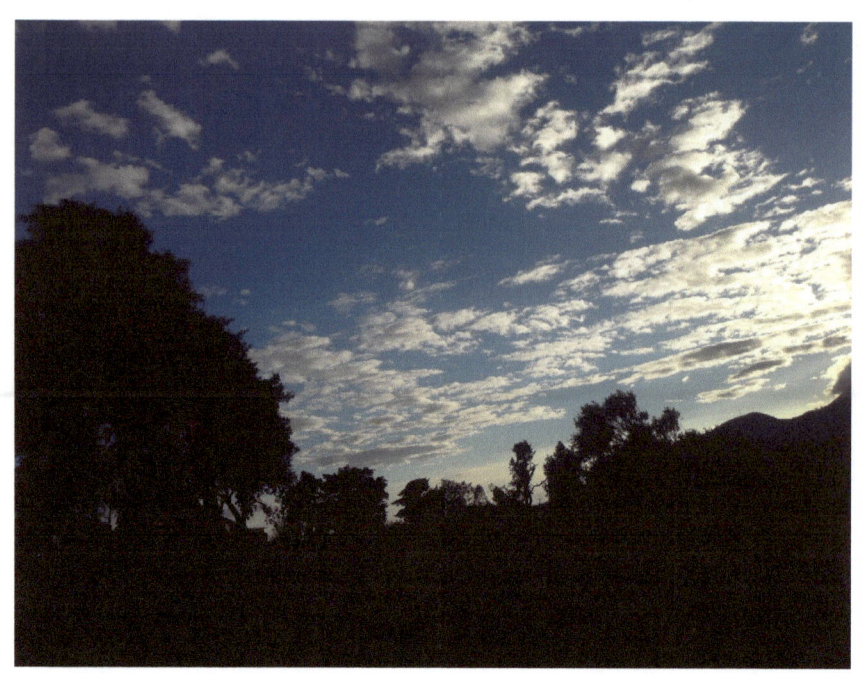

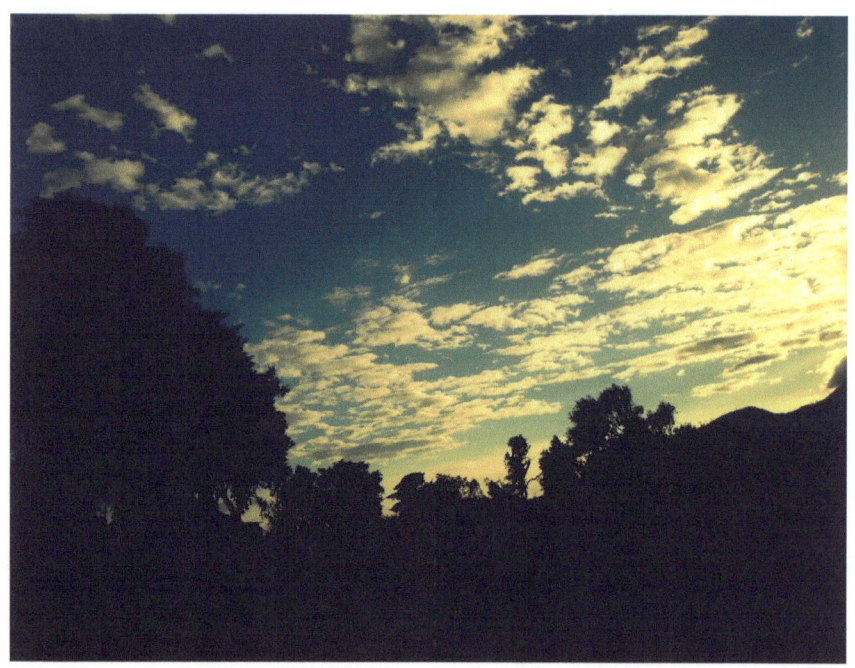

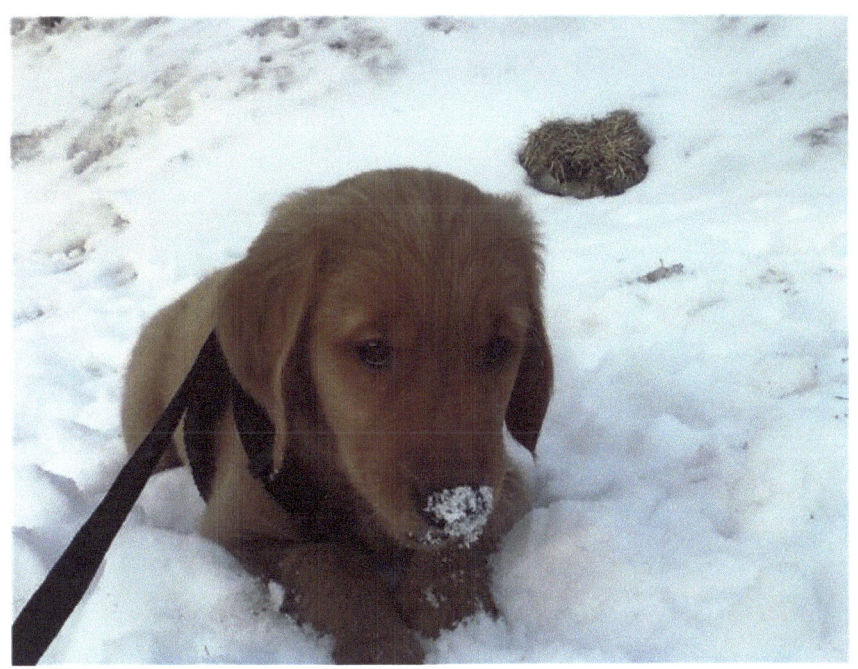

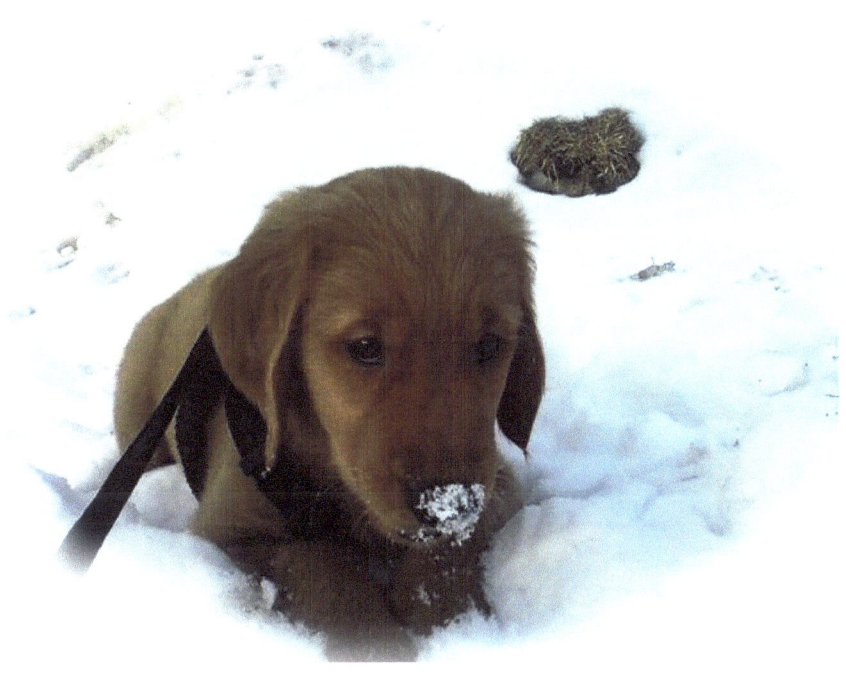

About The Author

Hello everyone! My name is Tony and I love nature. I have always been interested in having a healthy lifestyle and as time passed, I have found that a key element of this is getting in touch with our roots and what better way to do this than connecting with nature. I like to learn about many different things, I don't care about the subject as long as it is new knowledge. I am in quest to find my happiness and to do this, I try to see life in a spiritual way.

www.ingramcontent.com/pod-product-compliance
Lightning Source LLC
Chambersburg PA
CBHW040908180526
45159CB00010BA/2976